I0040319

YOUR BABY IS UGLY

BY JOHN JENNINGS

HOLON
PUBLISHING

Copyright 2023 John Jennings

Published by Holon Publishing

All rights reserved

ISBN: 978-1-955342-76-6

This book is sold subject to the condition that it shall not, by way of trade or otherwise, be lent, resold, hired out or otherwise circulated without the publisher's prior consent in any form of binding or cover other than that in which it is published and without a similar condition including this condition being imposed on the subsequent purchaser.

To my wife, Debbie, who has made the journey more fun and worth the ride. I could not have done any of this without you.

To all those business owners and leaders who are striving to build something beautiful.

CONTENTS

PROLOGUE

YOUR BABY IS UGLY – TEN TRUTHS BUSINESS OWNERS NEED TO HEAR, AND WHAT TO DO ABOUT THEM

First, let me confront the elephant in the room. Or maybe I should say the "ugly baby" in the room. The title. It's meant to be "tongue in cheek." It's a little catchy and, admittedly, a bit harsh. But it's just meant to be fun.

I believe that life should be fun. And when our business makes us miserable, we are probably doing something wrong, or doing the wrong thing. That's why I wrote this book. I hope that I can help you, the business owner or leader of your business, the person that has built a wonderful thing called "a business." But a business that might be stressing you out.

The purpose of this book lines up with my "why" or purpose statement:

> I believe that being a business owner or leader ought to be a source of great joy and personal fulfillment. I also believe that most are stressed and are experiencing anything but that. In fact, most are working way too hard for far too little. By bringing them simple tools and concepts, I help leaders overcome their challenges and find the personal fulfilment and joy they are looking for.

SO WHAT'S THIS "UGLY BABY" ABOUT?

For as long as I can remember, whenever I told someone bad news, I would often follow up the comment by saying something like "I know it feels like I just told you your baby is ugly, but I promise it's not that bad." I believe the expression comes from an "ugly baby" joke I was told as a child. But I digress.

When working with my clients or my past employers, I have often found myself helping the owner realize that something isn't quite right. These issues are usually blind spots, and they are all too common. I refer to these discoveries as "ugly baby moments" (that moment where you realize your business – your "baby" – has a problem). Examples of these include:

- Realizing that your business model won't work or deliver what is expected
- Recognizing that your workplace culture has problems
- Finding out your company isn't worth what you thought it was when you want to exit
- Realizing that you've been doing something wrong all along

Recently one of my clients had an "ugly baby" moment. I was working with a client in the home repair industry. We were comparing his financial numbers to industry standards. Something just wasn't right. We spent over an hour combing through the numbers and couldn't figure it out. It was time to end our session and I could tell he was frustrated. He knew I was writing this book, and what the title was about. I said, "Look, I know you just heard your baby is ugly, but we'll figure it out." As it turned out, he figured out that he wasn't marking some items up correctly. Essentially, he was leaving a lot of money on the table! Fortunately he found out after only being in business for about a year, and not many more frustrating years down the road.

THE STRUCTURE

As a business coach and strategic advisor, I work with many business owners. They are all passionate about their business. My role is to shed some light on what is going on – to help them take a hard look at their business. I never want to be the one who tells them there is a problem, but to help them recognize it for themselves. Following this format, I help my clients see the problem in their business, build a strategy to address it, and overcome. I look at it like this:

| Recognize | ⇒ | Respond | ⇒ | Resolve |

RECOGNIZE

In each chapter I share a story or two. These are simply to make you think and reflect. Do you see yourself in this story? Have you ever done something similar?

Honest self-evaluation can be difficult. The first step is to admit you have a problem. Taking that first step is difficult, but it's necessary.

I also hope these stories inspire you. They should help you realize that you aren't alone. That most businesses have challenges. That most leaders struggle at times, not knowing what to do or where to turn.

RESPOND

The true measure of a leader is how they respond to a problem. This is what sets you apart from those who do not lead well. There's an old adage attributed to many different people that states something to the effect that "no plan survives first contact with the enemy."

Your business may have had a great strategy. Your leadership may have been right on track. Your product may have been phenomenal. But unexpected twists and turns come along and knock you off your plans. Just in the past two decades we've seen a major terrorist attack, a bust in the tech sector, a recession, a housing crisis, challenges to our election processes, growing racial discord and a global pandemic. Any or all of these may have knocked your plans off course. It's how you respond to them that determines your success and the legacy of your business.

In each chapter I provide a few ideas for business owners to think about. These will not always apply to you. They are just that, ideas. I hope they give you some things to think about and to possibly put into practice.

I don't stop with business owners. I also provide a few ideas for those around them. For the coaches, advisors and critical team members that surround you. For them that choose to read this book, I want them to have ideas as well. These are some ways that they can help the business owner or leader address the issues they are facing.

RESOLVE

I hope to also show you that the ideas in this book produces results. If after a while, you have read this book, implemented changes, and do not see results, then it may not have been worth your time. I want you to see results! I believe the best way to help you is to share some of the results I have seen.

Sometimes my results aren't always what I would like them to be. Sometimes clients don't listen. Or there may be things I don't see as well. We use these times to learn, to be better, to have more success the next time.

After reading this book, I hope you have enormous success. I hope your baby is more beautiful than ever. I hope, truly hope, that your business success is wildly more than you hoped for. I hope your stories blow mine away! And if they do, I hope you'll let me know.

A FINAL THOUGHT

Most business books are too long and too boring. They usually have a few good chapters and then become repetitive. And; most of them paint rosy pictures to show that following their method is great. Some people hate reading business books because they make them feel guilty or insecure because their business isn't that great. And, having personal experience with some companies that have had books written about them, I know they often paint much better pictures and hide the ugly.

This book is raw and real, (but in a fun way). The stories are real, although names and some facts are distorted to protect identities. I hope you see yourself every now and then. I also hope you get some great ideas to make your business everything it can be, and more.

The responses and resolutions are real too. Every one of them comes from experiences I have led, or influenced, or personally witnessed. They all didn't work out perfectly, but most of them did eventually work out.

CHAPTER 1

YOUR BABY IS UGLY – WHEN YOUR BUSINESS MODEL ISN'T WORKING

You know them, I'm sure. Ugly baby moments. Those times when you must tell someone that what they are doing is not working. Sometimes it is a management style, other times it is a business concept. And then there are the times when you are not exactly sure what's wrong, but you know that whatever it is, it's simply not working.

Or maybe it's when you realize that your own baby is ugly. You take that long, hard look in the mirror and realize that the business you birthed has a problem. The business that is as integral to your life as almost anything you can imagine, this business – your baby – is deeply flawed.

Let me share with you a recent example of this. I get to work with clients in a variety of capacities. Sometimes I'm a coach; sometimes I'm an advisor. But other times I jump right in and help solve a problem. This is a story of one such time.

I had been working with a company as a strategic advisor for a few months. Initially it was an engagement to develop their strategic plan. Later, I worked with them to develop a model for holding each other accountable and I assisted them with taking the steps to carry out their strategy.

While working with them, I was tasked with helping this entrepreneurial organization move from an unscripted, "fly by the seat of their pants" model to a more refined, "well-oiled machine." The goal of this stage of my engagement was to document and lay out all the core processes that make up the "secret sauce" of the organization.

This company provided technology services to mid-size employers. Their products were somewhat expensive and had a long sales cycle. The CEO, David, believed that the key to retention was to show absolute cost savings in a real, measurable way. Their model included several ancillary products that brought additional value to their clients. From on-site support to custom software development, they had several creative services that were designed to save employers money.

The work was proceeding on task. I worked with the team to document sales and marketing processes, new client acquisition, client onboarding, customer service, billing, and many other processes. But there was one area of the business remaining. It was an area of the business that had largely been ignored in the previous couple of months and involved one of the ancillary services provided by the company.

The problem with this service was that no one seemed to want to have anything to do with it. Team members disavowed any knowledge or understanding of it. It had not been accepted by many clients either. Many said they had voiced their concerns, but the leadership had not listened.

On the other hand, this business segment was David's brainchild. He had sold the board on the idea a few years earlier. Consequently, he always spoke passionately about the benefit it could add to the business, the clients and their bottom line. The CEO asked me to dig into this segment and make recommendations. He was headed out of town on vacation and wanted to see the results of my analysis upon his return.

There was a consultant that ran this business segment for the company. I met him and immediately sensed some of the confusion. The consultant was an expert in sales but was not a detail-oriented operations person. Consequently, his energy was focused on how they could sell the service and not on how to effectively grow it. Unfortunately, the way it was designed, the program had little opportunity to make money. Furthermore, he was exhausted. He felt like he had been telling everyone that it wasn't working, but no one was listening. He knew this baby was ugly. But he had not been able to convince anyone.

This program represented the proverbial hamster on a wheel going nowhere. And the problem with it was that the more clients they sold, the more hamsters they were going to need to spin the wheel. All the time, spinning, and spending more and more money into oblivion.

It's not that this business was killing the company. But the truth was that it was generating a loss of at least $10,000 each month. And as we modeled the process, we realized that there was no hope for creating a profitable business model as it currently was designed.

We completed the process model and documented its shortcomings. Knowing that David would be back in town on Monday, we agreed to schedule a meeting with him to go over the results on Tuesday morning. We had identified key issues and why the program was not achieving the expected results, and we were fully prepared to demonstrate what we had learned.

Oh, the best laid plans... On Monday afternoon, the day before our scheduled conversation, David asked us if we had made any progress on the analysis. I began to speak up, to tell him that we would meet with him the next morning to share our results. But before I could fully defuse the situation, the consultant spoke up and essentially spilled all the bad news. It was one of those moments where you want to kick someone under the table; but there was no way to undo what had been done. The conversation came to an abrupt halt when the consultant told us he "was done" and didn't want to do this anymore.

"You're baby is ugly!" That's what the CEO had just been told. I spent the next few minutes talking everyone off the ledge and asked that we reconvene the next morning to go over what we had found. Everyone agreed, but David was upset with this news.

When we met the next morning, I didn't know if I'd still have them as a customer or not. The CEO was clearly upset about being blindsided. And truly, he had every right to be. He voiced his frustration at the meeting and asked what our solution was.

I told him the current model wasn't working. I laid out the facts and shortcomings of the current model. But I did not have a solution yet. Evidence from other companies demonstrated that we could develop a viable model, but we needed time to reinvent the program.

NOT THAT UNCOMMON

Over my career, I have worked with several businesses and/or teams that were not working. I have developed a reputation as a "turnaround guy" by going into broken teams and businesses, identifying what did not work, and then applying the changes needed to make the business a success.

However, for this to work, the leader of the organization must be willing to accept advice. All too often, business owners do not want to hear that what they are doing is not working.

On one occasion, I worked with a business owner that had a very compelling technical solution. It had the potential to profoundly change the business of healthcare. Innovations in healthcare can lead to a huge payday.

But the truth of this situation was simply that the business model he had developed was not going to work. In sales, you have to "follow the money". In other words, for a new idea to be adopted, you must be able to connect the savings generated with the source of the funds. This is especially true in healthcare. In this particular case, the savings/benefit went to one source (the patients), but the money had to come from another (the insurance agencies, aka "the payer"). Consequently, his model would never work.

Working with the business development team, we came upon a few ideas that would help correct this problem. But to do it would require a significant strategic change. He would have to drastically change his pricing model, and it would require a fair amount of product redesign. Sadly, he never heeded our advice, and was unable to bring his product to the market.

RECOGNITION. WHY IS THAT MIRROR SO CLOUDY?

Recognizing that our business model has problems has more to do with our ability to listen than anything else. As business owners we often do not listen to facts if they do not line up with our vision. As business owners, we must swallow our pride and be willing to listen to opinions that challenge our assumptions.

Most business owners are drivers. I use the DISC behavior assessment, and many business owners fall into the D or Dominant category. (*see sidebar*)

I first became aware of DISC after an assessment several years ago. Since becoming a coach in 2018, I have worked with TTI Success Insights (TTI Success Insights n.d.), a great company that has taught me how to apply the value of these assessments in real and practical ways.

Dominant people tend to suffer from similar traits. One of these is confirmation bias. Confirmation bias is one of several cognitive biases that we all struggle with. A cognitive bias is a systematic way of thinking where you apply input through a filter, often leading to very predictable results.

Confirmation bias occurs when you mostly interact with sources that support your prior conclusions. You favor what supports your opinions and dismiss what doesn't. (Wason 1972)

This bias demonstrates itself in several ways. One is that we tend to listen or watch news sources that match our political persuasion. Therefore, we discredit opposing ideas and never hear arguments that bring counterarguments to our own prejudices.

Another example of confirmation bias is that on social media, we tend to be fed content that fits our interests and existing opinions.

The DISC behavioral assessment is based on the 1928 work of psychologist William Moulton Marston. It identifies four distinct behavior types, Dominance, Influence, Steadiness and Compliance. Dominance identifies how you deal with decisions and problems, Influence identifies how you interact with people, Steadiness identifies how you deal with change and Compliance identifies how you feel about following rules.

I like it because it is easy to understand and to teach to my clients. It utilizes a two-dimensional graph, the horizontal access from left to right ranges from "reserved" (S and C) to outgoing (D and I). The vertical access from the top down ranges from "process oriented" (C and D) to "people oriented" (S and I).

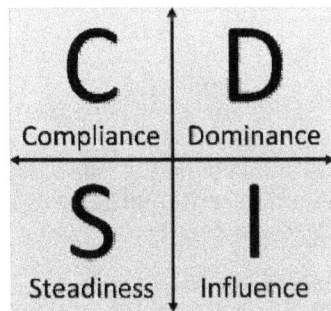

| C Compliance | D Dominance |
| S Steadiness | I Influence |

As a leader, confirmation bias can bring with it very troubling results. The most common scenario occurs when a leader solicits constructive criticism from his team. The team is usually tentative and not overly blunt, since he is the boss. As a result, the leader hears that things aren't so bad, and he just needs to make a few changes. Due to cognitive bias he believes everything is really okay and the team is aligned. Meanwhile his team is frustrated because they gave him feedback and he didn't listen.

I see it also happen when making decisions. Team members may share different options, but the leader almost always hears what he wants to hear. Confirming to himself that his opinion was the "right decision." He then believes everyone is on board, while everyone else feels like he is on his own planet.

The CEO in this chapter's first story did not hear the concerns from his team until it was put to him in a blunt and undeniable way in front of his whole team. The second story's CEO never heard any contrary opinions, and, unless he learns to listen, he may eventually lose everything.

LOOKING IN THE MIRROR

I wish I could say that I have never been guilty of confirmation bias. Several years ago one of my employers sent me to a nationally recognized leadership development program. Part of this program was an intense role-playing exercise where we were observed by the organization's staff through two-way mirrors.

After a day of activity, we had one-on-one debriefs with our instructors. I was told a couple of things that I just didn't agree with. One of the items pointed out to me was that in leading a discussion, I listened for what I wanted to hear, and then pressed ahead once I heard what I wanted to hear. I denied that it had happened, until they showed me the video. And yes, right before my very eyes, was a clear demonstration of confirmation bias. I truly did not believe was a problem. But it was.

WHAT'S A LEADER TO DO?

1. Listen, truly listen.

I will talk a lot about the need for leaders to listen in this book. If there's one magic answer to solve many problems of leaders, it is to listen more and listen actively. But to offset confirmation bias, there is another important step. The leader should play back what they heard to their team to confirm that they understand what was said.

Another term for confirmation bias is "selective hearing". My wife has accused me of that on more than one occasion. When a leader struggles with confirmation bias, they will most likely not play it back accurately. In fact, they often "spin" the comments around to fit their beliefs. Whether their team members correct them depends much on the next point.

Leaders who effectively listen understand that there are varying levels of listening required for each situation. Sometimes we are just listening without focus. We refer to this level of listening as "tracking." We're following along, but not really paying much attention. The second level of listening is being engaged. We sometimes refer to this as "active listening." At this level we are truly in-tune with the other person and avoid distractions. The final level of listening is something attuned to "mindfulness." With this level of attention we are truly, solely, completely focused on what the speaker is saying. We block everything else out.

2. Don't shoot the messenger (and maybe even reward them).

Whenever a leader tells me that they routinely ask for feedback and no one gives it to them, there's usually one of two causes. Either they hear what they want to hear (confirmation bias) and don't change, or they have a bad habit of "shooting the messenger". One of my past leaders would make a big deal about how he would never do this and then proceeded to rail on anyone who brought a concern to them. I'm not sure what he considered "shooting", but it's like he thought an actual gun had to be involved. He obliterated any employees who were trying to give honest feedback. Thus, no one ever wanted to give him it.

Do you want people to be open and honest with you? Don't promise not to shoot the messenger, as that instantly makes people skeptical. Reward those that come forward with honest concerns, and I am not talking about a formal high-cost recognition program. Take them to lunch. Send them a note. Thank them publicly. These moves will build a culture where open, honest feedback is welcome.

I saw a leader recognize a team member for finding a mistake in their accounting practices. The company had been making the mistake for years, and it cost them a considerable amount of money. The leader did not dwell on the past mistakes or what it had cost them. He simply recognized the employee for finding the problem and fixing it. This set the example that the company was not out to blame those that made mistakes, nor those that brought them to their attention.

3. Compare objective results with subjective feedback.

When you are hearing (or being told) one thing, and results don't match, then there is a disconnect. Somewhere. If your team says everything is great, but financial results show something different, then there may be a problem. Look objectively at what can be measured (sales numbers, quality factors, Key Performance Indicators, or KPIs) and see if they correlate with what you are hearing from your team. If they are not aligned, you should dig deeper.

One client was reporting positive sales activity on a regular basis, but their results simply were not aligning with that message. It took a while for reality to set it. Once the CEO realized that the activity and results were not aligned, we refocused the sales organization and realigned activities with expected results. Before long, the team made the necessary changes, eliminated some non-performers, and began seeing the results that they expected.

ADVICE FOR THE EMPLOYEE/COACH/ ADVISOR

Telling your boss, client or friend that their baby is ugly can be very difficult — and potentially what we call a Career Limiting Factor (CLF). Here's my advice to those that want to give bad news but keep their job or relationship intact.

1. Speak from facts, not opinion.

When bringing concerns to the table, focus on facts. In my story above, when team members expressed concern about the program, it sounded more about opinions than facts. The CEO often dismissed their *opinion* because he did not believe they understood the concept. In fact, it may have even sounded more like whining than anything else. It wasn't until facts were presented to him that he understood that there were real problems.

What types of facts matter? Numbers usually say it best. Whether it's financial (dollars being lost), time (how many hours are wasted), or feedback (customer or otherwise), these indicators are hard to argue against. And if the CEO argues against them, ask what they would like to see. Then come back and present them. Numbers and figures are the friend when presenting a fact-based argument.

2. Do not make it personal.

Here is a secret to working with business owners or CEOs: Everything is personal. When you express a concern about their idea, they take it personally. If you question the quality of the service provided, it's personal. If you question their strategy, you are questioning their ability to discern what is best for the organization. So, you should expect some pushback.

Some things I have seen business owners react most negatively to are the company name, brand, or logo. These things are the most personal of all. Tread lightly in these areas. Besides, these tend to be seen as opinions, not facts (see #1 for reminder).

I had a client who had a very long mission statement. It had a lot of filler words. I was working with them on some marketing ideas. While I wasn't hired to rewrite their mission or vision, I made the mistake of questioning one of the filler words in the mission statement. That was a mistake on my part. And the owner certainly let me know why *that* word was very important. I may have disagreed, but at that time it was not worth trying to change his mind.

Most business owners will initially have a knee-jerk reaction like this. Remember, you may have just told them, even if with facts, that their baby is ugly. So there is the potential for a very negative reaction.

3. Offer support.

Most business owners love to solve problems. This is another trait of the high-D Dominant leader. Most leaders reach their level of success, in part, due to their ability to solve problems. If you try to tell them what they need to do, they will naturally disagree. In fact, if you bring a good idea to the table immediately, it might get shot down because it was not their idea.

Business owners often want to be the people who figure it out. They *need* to find the solution. Therefore, you need to offer your willingness to support them. They love having a team to support them, and you will get your chance to share your idea later.

I once had a meeting with the CIO of one of our most important clients, a large federal agency. I flew to Washington, D.C. for the meeting and was not sure what topics would be on the table.

During the discussion he asked my opinion of one particular project. This one was his pet project, but I saw it as an ugly baby. The project was over-engineered, terribly expensive, and the technology equivalent of putting "lipstick on a pig."

Thinking quickly on my feet, I answered him this way. "The technology is state-of-the-art, very impressive. But, as a businessman, I don't think I could justify the return on investment (ROI). But I am sure we can figure that out."

I believe this was actually a very effective answer. I spoke from the perspective of facts, not opinion (#1, ROI being a measurable indicator). Remembering that this is personal, I scratched his ego, by complimenting the technology (#2). And I offered support by stipulating that I was sure we could figure it out (#3).

RESOLVE – RESOLUTION DRIVES RESULTS

David, the CEO with the ugly baby, accepted the fact that the program wasn't working as designed. The consultant resigned, and for a few months, they decided to focus on other things. This allowed opinions to soften, and moods to improve; it provided an opportunity to take a look at it with a fresh perspective.

About six months later, David spoke to me about his desire to get the program back on track. I offered to take on the task of redesigning and relaunching the program. After all, I have a reputation as a turnaround guy.

We spent about three months analyzing the results and understanding what was working and not working. Through our research we decided on a new path. We broke off some relationships and developed some new ones. Over the next six months we redesigned and relaunched the service. Within a year, we expect to be breaking even or generating a modest monthly profit. Furthermore, clients are benefiting from the program, and we are generating positive cash flow for the company.

But none of this would have been possible without having the "ugly baby" conversation. And while this one did not play out exactly the way I normally would have liked. In the end, we successfully turned things around.

And now, that ugly baby is rather cute.

CTA – WHAT'S YOUR BUSINESS GROWTH SCORE?

Are you interested in learning where you need to focus in order to improve your business? I can help you out there...

Your answers to the questions will be confidential and used only to help seek clarity in those areas.

This short assessment is *FREE* and will only take you about 3 to 5 minutes to complete by answering questions focused on the 5 main areas of business:

- CLARITY
- EFFECTIVENESS
- GROWTH
- SALES
- LEADERSHIP

At the end of the assessment, you will be given an overall score out of 100 as well as individual scores for each of the 5 main areas of business. You will also get a personalized report that breaks down your scores.

CHAPTER 2

NEITHER YOUR WAY NOR THE HIGHWAY? WHEN NO WAY IS THE RIGHT WAY

I have described myself as a "turnaround guy." I secured this reputation early in my career from some fairly simple projects. I had a knack for fixing problems others had overlooked and developing creative software solutions that were not apparent to others. My big break came when I got the chance to take over a failed project.

The project that was failing was a mid-sized, multi-year software project. And it had already developed the reputation of being an "ugly baby" before I got involved. As with many projects in the corporate world, there were many places where you could point the blame. In my opinion, the root cause of this problem in this case was the ego of leaders who saw no way but their way to solve a problem. When others disagreed with them, it got even uglier. Eventually, I had a chance to bring a new and better solution to the table.

This story takes place long before my days as a business coach. I was a programmer on a team at our local utility. This was late 80s, so we were still developing on mainframe computers. Programming languages such as COBOL were the norm. Very little custom software development was done in those days. The typical approach was to buy a software package, and modify the code to meet your needs.

While I was learning the ropes and completing small projects, there were some larger initiatives going on around me. I was not involved with any of them, but I heard rumblings of frustrations. One particular project was a management system being developed for one of our operations departments. This project was being led by a seasoned project manager along with an experienced systems analyst. This duo had already led the successful implementation of this same software for two other business units.

When this business unit indicated they needed a work management system, the corporate IT leadership decided that this existing, bought-and-paid-for software package would be their solution. The dynamic duo team went out to the user community and began to spec out the customizations that needed to be made.

Unfortunately, most of the user community did not feel they were being asked what they needed. They felt like they were being told how they were to use this software. When they voiced concerns, the response was that this was the official work management system for the company, endorsed by the corporate IT leadership, and that was that.

Months of work went into customizing the software. They set up a demo for the department leadership to see the new system. Meanwhile, a new vp of the department had come on board, and this was his first chance to see the software. The system was rolled out with much fanfare, to an underwhelmed audience. In fact, they were an irate, unhappy audience that refused to accept the software that was clearly not designed to meet the needs of their business.

The collective groan of frustration was heard throughout the IT department. Meetings were held; voices were raised. We all knew something was going on. This group turned down the collective expertise of the IT department questioning the wisdom and technical knowledge of the team.

The IT leadership had such contempt for this department. They described them in derogatory terms using terms like "juvenile" and "selfish." Some of the IT leaders wanted to deny them the ability to even have the system they needed. Others wanted to double down and force the solution on them.

Meanwhile, on my team, we also had a new leader. He was a very innovative, free-wheeling, creative thinking type of manager. He was just the type of leader that might get a guy like me in trouble because, whenever two creative spirits join forces, we tend to shake up things. He took charge and declared that we would start over and do it right this time. The systems analyst on the project refused and actually resigned. That's when I received the tap on my soldier. "John, here's your chance to step up a level." Naïve and excited, I took the plunge.

What I did not know, and did not find out for a few weeks, was that the project leader was also planning to leave. So just as we were getting our requirements gathering stage going, she submitted her resignation.

I had an idea, but it was a risk. I talked to one of my mentors. With his encouragement, I met with my new manager, who had just appointed me to the systems analyst role, and asked him if I could step up to the project leader role. It was a daring move. I promised him that if I got in over my head, I'd let him know. Or if I couldn't see that I was overwhelmed, he could let me know, and I would listen.

He agreed. Thus began a journey that would last for the next couple of years. I took a completely different approach to the project. I gathered requirements, spending weeks in the field learning how they conducted their business. I developed a data model of all the information they needed. We took the concept to both the business unit and IT leadership. There was a great deal of skepticism, but somehow we sold them on developing a software package from scratch. It was the first time in the company's history that they would do this. And it was one of the most successful projects I ever led.

And it all started by rejecting the leadership's demand to do it "their way," and by listening to what our customers actually needed.

IT HAPPENS WITH EXTERNAL CUSTOMERS TOO

Another company I worked with was led by a very intelligent man. He had several patents to his name and was able to break down technical challenges like no one I have seen. He developed an impressive data-driven software for a very needy market. His approach was unique and it had the potential to transform the market. He discovered new ways of storing and moving data. It was truly an ingenious solution.

Working in a business development role, my job was to find potential customers who could utilize the software's capabilities. On more than one occasion I found a hot prospect that liked some aspect of the platform. One time, a large not-for-profit organization put a bid out for a data transition project. What they were looking for was nearly an exact match to the backbone of this system. All we would need to do was make some changes to the inputs and outputs, and redesign how the data flow was triggered. In my opinion, it was a

15

slam dunk.

But the owner put his foot down and said he wouldn't do it. If they weren't going to use it the way he designed, then he wasn't going to sell it to them. He refused to even consider the possibility of this multi-year, multi-million dollar project. The irony here is that this business had virtually no sales and he had investors wanting to see a return. This was a big opportunity for the product, but his arrogance prevented him from moving forward.

I wish I could say that this one the only time that happened with him, but his arrogance prevented a lot of good things from happening.

WHY DOES THIS HAPPEN?

Ultimately this comes from an enormous need for power and control. Many in leadership suffer from this malady. In fact, the need for power and control is often what drives a person into leadership.

On the DISC profile, we often see this with high D leaders, especially in those leaders with a high D and high C combination. This desire for both being the decision maker (D) and following the rules (C), can be a vicious combination when you put them in a leadership position with little accountability.

I am not saying that all high Ds are dispassionate, out of control and power hungry. Behavior is just one dimension. If you truly want to find a leader with this problem, you need to look at what drives them as well.

Eduard Spranger discovered that we had six categories of human motivation and drive. If you have taken any type of assessment that identifies what motivates you, you probably have been exposed to his concepts. The six driving forces are:

- Theoretical – a passion for discovering the truth

- Utilitarian – a need to achieve a return on your investments

- Aesthetic – a passion for perfect form and harmony

- Social – a high value placed on the love of people

- Individualistic (aka "political") – a passion is to achieve position and use that power

- Traditional – a desire to seek out the highest meaning of life, to achieve a system for living. (Eduard Spranger 2013 (original 1928))

The value that we are most interested in this context is the "Individualistic." Spranger also referred to this person as the "Political." Their primary driving force is the attainment of position and power.

Utilizing behavior assessments from TTI, I have my clients take the Talent Insights Assessment. This instrument measures both behavior with DISC and determines where they score

I once worked for a business owner that fit this description to a tee. We had the opportunity to take the DISC assessment at a training session. He scored a 95 on the D scale (out of 100). As soon as he saw his score, he shouted, "I win, see, I win!!" He obviously didn't understand the concepts of balance and adaptation when it comes to our behavior.

12 Driving Forces®. When these two measures are put together, we can identify traits that lead to a strong thirst for power. (TTI Success Insights n.d.)

In general, when we see a high D combined with a high score on the "Individualistic" scale, we know that we have a high potential for a power-hungry leader. These are just the types of leaders that may demand "my way or the highway." And as the title of the chapter suggests, the right way is probably something in-between.

WHAT'S A LEADER TO DO?

It's easy to read the previous section and assume that there is nothing you can do. Some people are just "wired that way." And to some degree, that is true. But even when you are driven to act a certain way due to innate behaviors and desires, you can still learn to modify your actions and adapt to your surroundings. The effective leader does just that.

1. Recognize where you are.

Complete a behavior assessment. . My personal favorite is DISC. Or to be more specific, my personal favorite is the TTI Talent Insights Assessment, measuring both DISC and Eduard Spranger's Driving Forces®. (To purchase this assessment, find the instructions at the end of the chapter).

There are other quality assessments. The Predictive Index is comparable, but doesn't necessarily identify driving forces. The

"Captain" or "Maverick" profiles are likely to have this issue. Likewise, we would probably look at the Enneagram Challenger (the number 8) as someone with these same traits.

Whatever assessment you choose, if it demonstrates that you are a headstrong, driving, self-confident, forceful, confrontational, decision maker, then there's a good chance you are at-risk for this particular blind spot.

Of course, don't assume that because you have a specific trait or style, you should resign to behaving this way. We can all learn to manage our behaviors, once we are aware of them, which leads to the next point.

2. Learn to adapt, but not change.

I had a client with a combination of the high D and high C traits. She was the COO of the company. Her attitude was, "Why go home if there's still work to do?" For instance, she didn't understand employees who had a desire to attend school activities, or those who had other interests outside of work.

She constantly butted heads with the sales director. He was the exact opposite style, a high I. He was a family man with a small child. And his style was casual and engaging, a great salesman.

One day I stopped in to talk to her. She said she was exhausted; so I asked her why. She said that the sales director had been in the office all day. She tried to act like him in order to improve their relations. It was frustrating and exhausting.

She was trying to change herself to be *like* him. What she should have done is learn to adapt and work *with* him.

Adapting is sort of like the chameleon. They don't change shape, or DNA. They don't become a different animal. But in certain situations, such as changes in body temperature or mood, they adapt to the environment.

A leader needs to read his audience and communicate in the most effective way possible. For example, I have a client who is the CEO of her company. She is a creative leader, always looking for innovative approaches. Her CFO plays by the rules and speaks matter-of-factly. He may send an email that says something like "Don't call this person, just FYI." My client does not take kindly to being told what to do. Over time, the CFO learned to adapt. He would write "Take a look. If I were you, I might ignore this one." It's amazing, but a slightly different tone and word choice, and she was okay with the message.

3. Listen for alternative opinions.

In the story about the software project at the utility company, the IT leadership was completely condescending to the department and its user community. The IT leadership had an attitude of "be happy we are *giving* this to you." This arrogance was also part of the problem.

I referred to cognitive biases in Chapter 1. Confirmation bias comes in here as well. One method of overcoming our cognitive biases is to intentionally ask for and seek out alternative ideas. Purposely listen to the person that disagrees with you. Bring in third parties that aren't intimidated by your stature and will give you the straight-talk unfiltered opinion. Conduct focus groups or hire a facilitator to glean input from your team.

ADVICE FOR THE EMPLOYEE/COACH/ ADVISOR

Leaders like this do take bad news well. You cannot simply tell him his baby's ugly, not that you ever should! If you don't want to be shown the highway, you need an effective strategy for allowing them to adjust their thinking. This is not the type of leader that takes subtle hints. Nor can you bulldoze them into changing.

There are three keys to changing this leader's mind. If you follow this strategy, you have a good chance of walking away not only with your job, but also with a decision to move forward with your ideas.

1. Appeal to their ego.

The strengths of this leadership style include being straightforward, confident and direct. But in some situations, this comes across as arrogant and combative. When bringing a new idea or concern to them you must appeal to this trait. That does not mean that you "suck up" to them and try flattery. No, this leader recognizes superficial flattery and would be offended by it. But they do appreciate recognition of their strengths.

In the case of the IT project that needed to go in a new direction, we had to get the IT leadership on board with the new approach. If you remember, they had gone out on a limb and prescribed a solution without listening to the client.

In this situation we appealed to the vice-president's desire to be seen as an innovative leader in the industry. When we shared our proposal we pointed out that this would be the most innovative project we had taken on as a department. Additionally, we would stand out among other companies and would be seen as an innovative leader in the corporate IT community.

This approach worked. Our vice president was on board with trying something new. But it was critical to approach it the right way, or we would find ourselves with changes to our direction that might not be what we wanted.

2. Present them with options.

Dominant leaders see themselves as results-oriented and decisive. And while that is a great trait, you do not want them wreaking havoc with your plans. So be careful here. Remember, when you take a problem or proposal to this type of leader, they are going to want to solve it. They need to be able to make a decision.

I've been tempted in the past to take only one option to this type of leader. When you only take one option to them, they will *create* the second option. And often that second option is "No!" Unfortunately, I have made this mistake on more than one occasion.

Read the sidebar about how one client changed his communication style with his leader and it totally transformed his business and their relationship.

In the case of the IT leadership, we presented a couple of options to move forward. One of those options was to stay the course with the original plan. The second option was to move forward with this new approach. Since we had

One of my clients discovered the secret to effectively communicating with a directive leader. We were exploring some of the challenges he was facing and he told me how frustrating it was that 80% of his decisions were overridden by his boss, the president of the company.

We discovered that he tended to send emails that explained the situation and presented what he believed to be the best answer. In many cases, he had already taken steps to implement the approach he chose.

The problem with this approach is that the president always saw it as a problem to solve. And so, he almost always changed the decision, because – well – that's just what he did.

The solution was to change his writing style. He presented a quick summary of the issues and followed with an "FYI" of the decision that had been made. The president's responses became responses of affirmation instead of ones changing the direction of the team. A simple answer to a frustrating problem.

appealed to their ego (Step 1), we knew that there was very little chance that we would be going with "stay the course" option. This was a huge win.

3. Ensure the win.

Another trait of this type of leader is the need to win. They are very competitive. And so, along with presenting your desired option, you need to provide evidence and support that you will be successful. Appealing to their ego only works if they are confident that you will come out with the win.

For that reason, you must be very succinct and direct when you present your idea. They are impatient and do not like wandering presentations.

In the case of our IT project, we put together a very professional, slick presentation. This was during the early era of the personal computer, and word processing programs were fairly new to our environment. We put together an attractive, easy to follow document that was very impressive to the leadership team.

More than two decades later, while in a business development role, I realized that my years of selling ideas to leadership were a perfect training ground for the skills needed to do my job well.

CLOSE THE DEAL

Working with this type of leader can be a challenge. This is one of those times where we use the phrase "managing up." If you adapt your style and present things in the right way, your challenging, dominant, "my way or the highway" leader can become your biggest supporter.

But here is one very important point. You must be able to close the deal. Remember, you appealed to their ego and promised a win. You must deliver.

In my case, we did. The project was on-time and on-budget. We delivered a custom developed application that served their needs for many years to come. I remember talking to someone at the company nearly 20 years later, and they told me that parts of that system were still being used.

CTA – DISCOUNTED ASSESSMENT FOR "UGLY BABY" READERS!

Are you interested in learning more about your personal behaviors and motivators?

Self-awareness is the first component of Emotional Intelligence. To be self-aware is to have a deep understanding of your behaviors, strengths, weaknesses, needs and drivers.

People who have a high degree of self-awareness recognize how their feelings affect themselves, others and their job performance.

The performance of individuals and teams can be greatly enhanced through increasing self-awareness and we achieve this through some of the most powerful behavioral assessment tools available today.

Combining both behaviors (DISC) and 12 Driving Forces (motivators) into one integrated report, Talent Insights explains the HOW and the WHY behind a person's actions.

Scan to order a Talent Insights Assessment ($97.50 for readers – instead of $195)

CHAPTER 3

WHEN YOUR MAIN THING IS NOT THE MAIN THING.

One of the earliest pieces of advice I received from a mentor was to always be able to quantify my value to the organization. He would say, "Everyone should understand what their fully burdened cost to the organization is." "Fully burdened" is a fancy accounting term meaning your salary plus all your benefits, including vacation and paid time off. It's not unusual to estimate the value of these "burdens" to be worth at least 50% of your hourly rate. For example, if your hourly rate is $40, your fully burdened rate might be as high as $60 per hour.

Furthermore, he would say, each employee should be able to look at any period of time and ask themselves, "Did my employer get their money's worth out of me?" You might have some hours of the day where you recognize that this didn't happen. Even some days you may realize that you didn't contribute your value. We've all had them. The day when you were unable to make progress on your goals, or perhaps keep getting sidetracked with unimportant items.

But over time, you should always be able to look in the mirror and, with confidence, state that your employer did get their money's worth from you. When I was an employee, I would occasionally think about this. I would quantify some of the value I brought to them. I almost always was able to make a direct correlation from my costs to the benefit I gave them. I believe that mindset is part of what kept me employed for many years.

THE BUSINESS OWNER'S DILEMMA

I find that this comes up sometimes when business owners do not focus on the most important activities. As coaches we often remind people to "keep the main thing, the main thing." One way I help them see this is through understanding the value of their time.

But this activity doesn't always work for business owners. Some do not even take a regular paycheck. When calculating an hourly rate, they often cannot even calculate everything to determine their fully burdened cost.

One of my clients was an independent salesperson, deriving his revenue from the contracts he brought to ecommerce providers. He hired me at a time when he was frustrated with his pipeline and time management issues. He felt he couldn't get enough done in the day and subsequently was not able to bring in enough new clients to sustain his business.

I started working with him on some standard time management activities such as time blocking and focusing on his areas of awesome. But these did not solve the problem.

Eventually we measured the activities he was performing each week. We then looked at the value of each of these items. To his surprise, we found that he was wasting a lot of time on low-value activities.

I remember vividly this day we sat outdoors at a coffeeshop, looking at his income reports. He had numerous pages of data, showing how much he was earning from each client. His top clients provided him with a nice income. But as we flipped through the report, we saw very modest levels of income. By the end we had saw a lot of clients that were generating something closer to pennies than dollars.

Let me give another example. Let's say that Ronald wanted to earn $200,000 annually. This translates to an hourly rate of $100 per hour. Any time that he spent on something of less value is devaluing his time.

After conducting this activity, we found Ronald spent at least 25% of his time dealing with small accounts. On average, each time he solved an issue for a small account, it took at least one hour of his time. But one-third of these small accounts delivered less than $50 per month in revenue. On average, he spent one-fourth of his time working for less than $20 per hour. And for some of his accounts, he was effectively earning for less than minimum wage!

I see this in entrepreneurial CEOs as well. One of my clients is constantly thinking out into the future. His entrepreneurial spirit is largely the reason behind the company's early successes. He is an innovative, versatile, leader who brought the company to the market with his skills of leadership, inspiration and vision.

But as the company grows, those skills have to be deployed in new ways. The "fly by the seat of your pants" mentality that helps you adjust, pivot, and create in those early days, can be disastrous if you grow too much too quickly. Entrepreneurial CEOs have to learn the keys of balance and prioritization.

The ugly baby truth that this leader needed to understand was that sometimes he was standing in the way of their company's success. While he wants to be the CEO, leading the company with a strategic vision, he finds himself returning to what made him successful in the early days of the company. He gets involved with sales, he constantly reinvents the strategy and wanders away from the company's core values and vision. And while that gives him a great deal of personal satisfaction, it does not give the company what it most desperately needs. Furthermore, it leaves the employees and the shareholders, frustrated with a CEO that constantly is in the weeds, instead of one that is casting a vision.

WHY DOES THIS HAPPEN?

One of the models I often show a client is something called the "Three Eyes of the Business Owner." Michael Gerber articulates this well; in his book EMyth Revisted. There are three roles that a business owner finds themselves involved in. These are the Technician, the Manager and the Entrepreneur or Visionary.

In the role of technician, the CEO is performing the tasks of the business. If the business is a plumbing business, he is working as a plumber. If it's a digital marketing firm, she's developing the website. While this is common in a small company, it is not sustainable as the company grows. Whatever the case, we describe this type of work as working in the business rather than on the business. The CEO is essentially working at the hourly wage of the technician they could hire to do this work. In some cases, this might be a substantial amount, but it is not the level at which the CEO should be performing.

In the role of manager, the CEO is reviewing and analyzing the performance of the company. This may involve reviewing financial reports and sales pipelines. It involves monitoring the company's Key Performance Indicators (KPIs) to ensure performance standards are met. At this level, the earning power of the CEO is limited to the hourly wage of a person hired to perform this function.

When the CEO is in the role of entrepreneur or visionary, they are looking out for the future of the business. Their minds are set on bigger ideas, longer-term opportunities and solving big problems. In this role, great ideas are generated, and great inventions are dreamt of. In this role, the earning potential of the CEO is virtually unlimited.

In most small businesses, we find that the CEO is focused primarily on working in the technician role. Even though they may deny it, we typically see CEOs in small businesses spending at least 80% of their time doing so. They spend 15% of their time in the manager role. That means they are only spending their time on the most valuable tasks about 5% of the time. That's only a few hours per week! And we wonder why so many small businesses fail and why so many small business CEOs burn out. They say they are working way too hard for much too little.

> "If your business depends on you, you don't own a business—you have a job. And it's the worst job in the world because you're working for a lunatic!"
> — **Michael E. Gerber, The E-Myth Revisited**

WHAT'S A LEADER TO DO?

If you remember, that last sentence comes straight from my "Why" statement. I believe most business owners are working way too hard for much too little; and I have built my business around changing that paradigm.

1. Flip the script.

The first thing I tell CEOs who are struggling with the technician role is to "flip the script." Instead of the ratio of 80% technician, 15% manager, 5% visionary that we see in so many leaders, we need to operate something like 5% technician, 15% manager and 80% visionary. That may seem impossible; and to be fair, it may be impossible in the short term. So set your sights on the time when you can spend four out of five days on being the visionary, and only one day a week on everything else.

Let me ask you this. What type of ratio do you think Steve Jobs had when he was at Apple? I don't know, but I'm sure that when they created the iPhone he had long ago put away his soldering iron and hadn't touched a line of code in many years.

This isn't easy. It is especially difficult when you truly love, truly have a passion, for the product or service you provide. And let's face it, there are some industries where it's not realistic – like doctors and lawyers for instance. For the masses, however, a CEO who wants to lead an entrepreneurial company, and to manage his time and finances more efficiently, needs to understand this concept and move in this direction.

How do you do that? One way is to focus on your Area of Awesome.

2. Find your Area of Awesome.

The "Area of Awesome" exercise is another activity I put my clients through. It is especially useful when they are dealing with working in the business instead of on it. I have my friend, mentor and coach extraordinaire, Rich Scott, to thank for teaching this exercise to me.

We start by having them list everything they do in a typical week. This doesn't need to be too granular, but it does need to capture the big buckets of information. This might include things like:

- Respond to customer communications
- Make sales calls
- Review financials
- Resolve customer complaints
- Schedule resources for the week
- Staff meetings
- One-on-one meetings with direct reports

Second, we categorize them into four areas:

- AWKWARD - Things you are not good at doing, don't like doing, and have low value

• ADEQUATE - Things that you are okay at doing, but still don't like doing.

• ACCOMPLISHED - Things that you are good at doing and they bring a modest value.

• AWESOME - Tasks of great value, that comes naturally and easy for you and generates energy

Finally, I have them go back and indicate which ones are technician roles (T), manager roles (M) and visionary roles (V). Here is an example from one of my clients:

AWKWARD	Bookkeeping/accounting tasks (T) Cold-calling executives at potential clients (T) Emails (T) Contract Reviews (M)
ADEQUATE	Reviewing financials (M) Staff meetings (M) Responding to customer questions/complaints (T)
ACCOMPLISHED	Training clients (T) Preparing for investors meeting (M) 1-on-1 meetings with staff (M) Strategy sessions (V) Social media strategy (M)
AWESOME	Branding & content creation (V) Sales conversations (T) Networking (T) Sales meetings (M)

For this client, we started with the Awkward category. I suggested that the first three awkward items could be eliminated. He has an accountant that can handle this work, cold calls are a waste of his time, and he could use a virtual assistant to help manage his email. The fourth item could be modified to have someone else review contracts and just present him with the summary. Then maybe that moves down a category or two, and becomes slightly more visionary.

Second, we also worked on moving almost all of the technician tasks off his plate except sales conversations. And we broke those into two categories. strategic accounts or partnerships (now more of a visionary role), and small accounts (which we moved off his plate).

Furthermore, we added a strategic component to sales meetings that focused more on filling the funnel than status reports of items in process.

When this progression is complete, this leader should go from a 80%-15%-5% role, to something more like 25%-35%-40%. It's not a purely visionary leader, but now two days a week he spends in the visionary role. He is surely going to be more impactful than he was before.

There are two key learnings from this example:

• Most CEOs put greater value on technician tasks than they should

• Most CEOs don't even think of making visionary tasks part of their daily schedule

Brian Tracy says that a business owner shouldn't do anything that someone else at a lower wage can do. That's a tall order. I find most business owners push back on this; but unfortunately, until they face this reality, their business will only grow as far as their capacity to make it happen on their own.

> Their business will only grow as far as their capacity to make it happen on their own.

Why is this so hard for a CEO to accept this role? Why do most CEOs of small businesses spend too much time in technician mode? They often struggle to realize that others can be more effective in doing some types of work. Two challenges I see all the time are the need for more delegation and its closely related concept of "good enough."

1. Delegate for "good enough."

Most leaders do not delegate enough because they do not think that the work will be performed to the same degree that they would do it. And my response to that is "so what." That just means you have an opportunity to coach and improve their performance. Until you can accept "good enough" and manage the team to improve performance to your level, you will never be comfortable with delegation.

And yes, I know some of you are rolling your eyes saying, "Good enough? In my industry there's no such thing!" Oh yes there is. Admittedly, "good enough" for a brain surgeon is different than "good enough" for a telemarketing firm or a landscaping business. But no matter what you do, how critical it is, how complicated it is— there is always a level of performance that is good enough.

There are many reasons leaders fail to delegate well. Many leaders don't think the task can be completed by anyone else, most don't want to take the time to teach the skills, and many don't know where to start.

That is why you need to follow an organized process for delegation. Delegation does not mean you send a text to someone and say "do it", or that you ignore things you don't want to do until someone else picks it up. Here are eight key steps to effective delegation:

1. Clearly define the task – People can't be expected to do something if you cannot explain it to them.

2. Identify the standards – Your delegate cannot be successful if they do not know the measures. You certainly cannot move the goalposts after you define them.

3. Determine the schedule – Like standards, time constraints are also critical to measure success. What timing is "good enough?"

4. Identify the correct person – Notice that we did not pick the person first. After you understand what has to be done, how well it must be done, and how fast it must be done. Now you can pick the right person for the job.

5. Choose the appropriate delegation style– A one-size fits all mentality will not work. Some will need greater hand-holding, while more seasoned staff may take it and run.

6. Discuss the role – I see many delegation attempts as a one-sided conversation. "Here's what you do. Come see me if you have questions." But do you mean it? When they have questions, do you help, or tell them "It's your role, figure it out?"

7. Manage the delegate – Note that this does not say to "solve any and all problems." But to be willing to assist when you see them in trouble. Have periodic check-ins to make sure they are on track. Do not necessarily wait until the deadline to see if they did the job.

8. Recognize the success – How often is this overlooked? You just managed to take something off your place. A team member is now handling the task. You feel great about things. Do you tell them? Do you recognize them? Do not miss this important step. It makes the next delegation go much easier.

ADVICE FOR THE EMPLOYEE/COACH/ ADVISOR

Did you ever just want to be the hero? As a child I dreamt of growing up to be the firefighter or policeman who rescued the cat in a tree or pulled the person out of burning building.

Helping a leader solve a major problem is as close as I'm ever going to get to being a hero. Leaders often face "disasters" on the work front. In fact, sometimes we call them "fire drills." Whether it's a project gone astray, the loss of a key employee or leader, or a product that is faulty and needs to be recalled, leaders have to deal with these and other issues on a regular basis.

1. Rush into the fire.

As a member of the team, you have an opportunity when these situations arise. It doesn't even have to be as dramatic as these examples . At almost any given time, your leader is wrestling with something that is stressing them out.

Here is your opportunity. But before you take action, do some research and practice this script.

Observe what is going on in your company or your team. Figure out what is causing the most pain for your leader. Chances are; they are trying to figure out a solution to one of these problems.

Remember the story about the management system in Chapter 2? That is a good example of one of these times. I took the loss of two key team members as a way to step into a leadership role and launch my career.

You are going to find out what is his number one problem. Furthermore, you are going to determine if there is a way that you can help. Chances are, if you are reading this book, then you have something within you that makes you that person who can step up and save the day.

Find a time to meet with your boss. This isn't during a casual conversation. Set up some time to talk to him. Request the meeting.

In that meeting, the script goes something like this. Tell your leader that you know that this is stressing them out. You have an idea and you would like to help solve their problem. Perhaps this means taking on a special project, or stepping in to fill a gap left by someone else.

If you want to truly make a difference, to be seen as a pivotal member of the team, then stand up, and volunteer to solve the problem. Remember the "ugly baby" in Chapter 1? The service offering was losing money. When the CEO decided to try the relaunch, I stepped up to be the guy to bring it to market.

The first key to success is this; demonstrate confidence. Your leader

No good deed goes unpunished....

Building a reputation as a person who can step in and solve the problem has cascading effects. I had developed a reputation as a problem solver. A "turnaround guy" of sorts. One day my boss comes standing at the door of my office with "that look" on his face.

"Are you up for a challenge?" he asked.

Nervously, I asked what was up. He told me that the performance problems in the new ERP system had risen to the C-suite at our company. And that I was tapped to lead a team to solve the problem. And, I had 90 days to figure it out.

Fortunately, this particular situation had a happy ending. In fact, we solved a problem that had been stumping the team for months. And we did it in a few weeks.

It was a little nerve racking at first. But just for a moment, we felt just a little bit like those first responders who ran into the fire in order to save the day!

needs to truly believe they can trust you to fulfill the mission. You are effectively "delegating yourself," taking that responsibility away from them.

And it doesn't stop there. (This is critical.) Tell them "I know this is a big leap for me, and I may be jumping in over my head. I want you to know that I'll let you know if I feel like I'm getting in too deep. As long as you promise to do the same if you see that I'm headed into rough waters." This statement does two things. It demonstrates your maturity and wisdom in not being over-confident; and it acknowledges that they have the right to pull the plug should problems arise, and that you are okay with this. You recognize that you may need a lifeline, and you are setting this up before you even begin.

There is, of course, no guarantee that your boss will take you up on this; but I have done this numerous times in my career. Sometimes it was a big step, such as stepping up to take on leadership of a whole department or team. Other times it was something simple like stepping in to help solve a software issue that was slowing down productivity. And on a couple of occasions, I had to use the lifeline. One time, I stepped up to take on management of a second team of software developers. It worked for a while, but when issues kept arising on both teams, I found myself unable to adequately lead two distinctly different teams. Fortunately, someone else in the organization had demonstrated leadership capacity during the months I was doing this, and she was able to step up and take the mantle of leadership on one of the teams.

2. Just do the little things.

Kurt Warner, the Hall of Fame Quarterback who overcame tremendous professional and personal battles, went on to become two-time NFL MVP and Super Bowl Champion. His sudden rise to greatness has very few parallels in any sport. One year before his ascension to the top of the NFL, he was playing football in the Arena League. One year before that, he was stocking shelves in a local grocery store.

The manager of the store credits Warner with great work ethic. He said that his aisle always looked perfect. Every can was perfectly lined up, every label facing the same direction. He made sure his aisles were perfect for the first customers that entered the store each day.

In an interview with Warner, he was asked why that was so important. He said, "The way you do the small things is an indicator of how you'll do the big things."

Small things are often the biggest nuisance for today's CEO. With email, cell phones, and social media, the CEO faces many distractions. Without some assistance, they can find themselves chasing down rabbit holes. One way you can help is to take some of the small things off their plate.

One of my clients is a CEO of a software company. She often finds herself in the weeds and unable to come up for air. She is fortunate to have another team member who is constantly on the lookout for this. Whenever she sees it happening she steps in and asks "What can I take off your plate?" For years this CEO resisted relinquishing control, but over time she came to recognize that this was the only way they were going to survive. More importantly, it was the only way *she* was going to survive.

FINDING OUT WHAT'S IMPORTANT

Remember the sales executive that was working for less than minimum wage for some accounts? He learned to prioritize where he was focusing his time. When issues arose with small accounts, he handed them off to the support team to handle. He learned not to sweat the small things and focus on his major accounts.

In doing this, he strengthened his relationship with his most important clients, and he lost a few of his smaller troubling ones. And that's okay. He learned to forgive himself for not being there for every small detail. Eliminating some of his smaller clients gave him the time to focus on serving his most valuable clients and to build his business. He increased his pipeline and brought more high-value prospects. Within a year his business was up 20%, and he had more balance in his life. He was enjoying his work and not burdened by clients that were costing him more than they were worth.

And the CEOs I talked about? Well, most of them are still works in progress.

CTA – ARE YOUR PRIORITIES IN LINE?

There are five essential priorities available to us. There is an optimal order to these priorities, and each one has its own currency, or way that it manifests itself. If we keep these priorities aligned properly, we will experience unprecedented success personally and professionally.

The old saying is still true: "As the leader goes, so goes the company." Organizations can only reach their desired levels of health, productivity and profitability if their leaders model attitudes and behaviors worth following. Leaders worth following are humble and hungry. They are characterized by their investment in personal and organizational growth and their commitment to keeping the right priorities in the right order. Companies known for their empowering culture hold fast to the following ordering of priorities:

First, we find that great leaders have a vision that's bigger than themselves. Secondly, they have the unique ability to be both humble and direct. Encourage and Empower those around them. Speak Truth while Confronting Reality They confront the brutal facts of today, yet keep an unwavering hope in the future (Jim Collins).

John Maxwell calls these Level Five Leaders. They balance:

- Heart and Head
- Encourage and Empower
- Humility and Courage
- Empathy and Directness
- Hope and Reality

Is your organization's priorities in the right order?

Scan to order The Prioritized Leader assessment ($75 for readers – instead of $150)

CHAPTER 4

OOO-OOH THAT SMELL. WHEN YOUR CULTURE STINKS.

"We work hard and play hard." That was the answer from the vice president of information technology. I was being recruited for a position at a Fortune 500 corporation. At the time I was quite happy in my current role, but there were few growth opportunities there, and I was looking forward to getting into a larger organization with lots of opportunities. This job was with a respected company that had a global presence. The upside of working at this company was endless.

But I soon found out what she meant by her statement. Yes, the employees at this company worked hard. That's never been a problem for me. I enjoy a good challenge. But in this organization the competitive nature of every position created a highly competitive environment where team members at every level were constantly striving to outdo one another. Every day felt like a battle. Leadership was constantly vying for power and position.

And the play hard part? Yes, periodically teams would go out after work for happy hour. They would have quite the good time. That is, until they woke up with a hangover the next morning. It was the same way at other gatherings, like the company holiday party or department picnics. Some of the parties reminded me of fraternity parties in college.

The culture of this organization was grounded in competition. Bloody competition. In this highly competitive culture, it seemed like we were constantly on one end of the spectrum or the other. Either we were diligently working hard for the company to deliver on our responsibilities, or we were completely letting our hair down and having a raucous time attempting to forget.

I saw this play out over several years. Entry level employees were contending to be on the "right project." Managers fought for key roles. There were even "teams" of managers that aligned under competing directors. We even used those terms, such as "Susan's team." And depending on who was in charge at the time, one director's team would have the upper hand on everything from leading key projects to gaining the top new talents entering the company.

COMPETITIVENESS GONE AWRY

One of the primary drivers that I see in unhealthy cultures is when competition gets in the way of achieving the greater goal. Healthy competition can build a thriving company. Unhealthy competition, however, can lead to a truly toxic culture.

This was never more obvious than with one client I was working with. The CEO and the vice president of sales were both born and raised in New England, and fit the stereotype of a highly driven "northerner." (Or Yankee, as we would call them in the south). Both of these men were high Ds on the DISC assessment. A high D means you exhibit a dominating, directive behavior when it comes to making decisions and solving problems. High D people also tend to be naturally more competitive. These people love to win. Nothing gives them more satisfaction than winning.

When you have two dominant personalities at the top of the organization, you are naturally going to have some disagreements. But with these two, disagreements turned into full-on shouting matches. They would go at each other like a WWF match. And it could go from a calm discussion to an all-out shouting match in a matter of minutes. They would talk – or shout – over each other, and nothing would be resolved.

If it would end there, that might be okay. But seldom would the issue be resolved there. Alliances would be formed. The VP of Sales would seek alliances from the other executives. The CEO would make sure that his other reports fell into line. And the issue wouldn't be resolved until one faction beat the other.

Another client was hiring a new CFO. The CEO was a very high D. (Close to 95 on the scale). The CFO candidate also tested as a high D. I told my client that as long as these were on the same page, they would work well together, leverage each other's strengths and push hard toward the goal. Together, the two could be unstoppable. However, when they did lock horns in disagreement, it may get ugly. Sure enough, about 8 months into his tenure, the CFO came to blows with the CEO. Fortunately, we were expecting this to eventually happen, and we worked through it with some finesse.

WHY DOES THIS HAPPEN?

Competition can be a great thing in organizations. Most sales teams thrive in competitive environments. When I led sales organizations, I would always try to create a healthy level of competition between the sales reps. We would have awards for meeting certain criteria. And salespeople that hit milestones would get special recognition and bonuses.

I've created healthy competition in other areas of business as well. In operations we recognized teams that completed projects on time. We would reward technicians that exhibited high levels of efficiency or had a low number of errors or callbacks. In a service department we created awards for employees who received positive feedback from customers.

Competition that is based on clear, definable, and logical measures is very effective. Competition that is subjective and driven by popularity and politics creates division and strife.

At a previous employer we would often say that you could recognize the people who got passed over for a promotion by the footprints on their back. It was very common to see people take every opportunity to get a leg up on their competition. Why? Largely because of the concept of winners vs. losers, and the presence of a *scarcity mindset*.

WINNERS VS. LOSERS

Highly competitive environments also reward a certain style of individuals while holding back others. Employees with high D personalities will typically thrive in these environments. While those who follow the rules or try to provide quality work will typically blend in and not advance at the same rate.

By constantly rewarding those who are highly competitive, these organizations end up with unhealthy cultures based on an environment of beating each other, instead of having a healthy culture of helping each other.

Organizations with a heavy emphasis on "winning" have an unstated culture point that if you aren't the winner then you are a loser. Healthy organizations recognize that people bring value in multiple ways, not just by being the person at the top of the pyramid.

This type of competitive spirit is great for those hyper competitive individuals. But since almost one-half of society is not wired this way, it creates an uncomfortable, and perhaps even hostile, culture for a large percentage of your team.

ABUNDANCE VS. SCARCITY

Fundamentally, one of the biggest differences between healthy and unhealthy competition is on how we view "winning." An abundance mindset leads a person to the belief that there is an endless amount of resources in the world. There is enough for each of us to get our piece of the pie.

A scarcity mindset, on the other hand, views the world as limited in resources. When one person wins, another person automatically loses. There are no win-win scenarios.

When it comes to a competitive corporate culture, if the mindset of the team is based on the scarcity framework, team members will naturally fight for their own personal cause. When a person is wanting a manager position, he or she sees that one opening as scarce. Therefore, when someone else gets it, they see themselves as the loser. When the scarcity mindset rules the day, everything becomes a win-lose situation.

WHAT'S A LEADER TO DO?

1. Turn your focus inward.

In his book *The Infinite Game*, author Simon Sinek encourages business leaders to not focus on what the competition is doing. Instead, build highly effective teams by focusing on improving ourselves and our employees.

He describes two ways of thinking, having an infinite mindset or a finite mindset. The most successful leaders recognize that business is an infinite game, constantly evolving and never ending. Those who focus on business as a finite game are instead concerned more about short term issues and have a win vs. lose attitude.

It's sort of like the difference between playing tennis and playing golf. I am a decent golfer and a terrible tennis player. Tennis is a finite game. There's a definite score, definite rules. When you (or in my case, my opponent) scores enough points, they win. No doubt. No question about it.

But in golf it's different. Yes, I may compete against my playing partner. But more often than not, I am competing against myself. I'm trying to shoot a better score than my average. I'm trying to make the difficult shot that I couldn't make last time. I hope to hole more putts and hit more fairways. And since I'm not making a living at it, I can win or lose against my playing partner and still have a great time.

> "An infinite mindset embraces abundance whereas a finite mindset operates with a scarcity mentality. In the Infinite Game we accept that "being the best" is a fool's errand and that multiple players can do well at the same time."
> — **Simon Sinek, <u>The Infinite Game</u>**

This is very much aligned with the mindset of abundance and scarcity described earlier. If I believe there is enough "prize" to go around, then I don't focus on the exclusivity of winning. When I play golf, I hope that each of us has a great time, hits lots of great shots, and enjoys our time on the course. If I "win," then that's just a bonus.

According to Sinek, one of the keys is to build trusting teams. This isn't easy. He says that it "starts by creating a space in which people feel safe and comfortable to be themselves." Fear, he says, is a powerful motivator, but it can force us to act in unhealthy ways — ways that aren't in the best interest of the organization.

Sinek's conclusion? "When leaders are willing to prioritize trust over performance, performance almost always follows. However, when leaders have laser-focus on performance above all else, the culture inevitably suffers." (Sinek 2019)

Business owners who focus solely on results, despite anything else, will likely see them in the short term. But to the long-term detriment of their team and their company.

41

2. Develop emotionally intelligent teams.

Emotional Intelligence (often abbreviated "EQ") is a key factor in building healthy teams with healthy cultures. We know that the most effective leaders are those who develop and build high levels of EQ on their team. A team with a high EQ will out-perform those with average or low levels of EQ every time.

There are several factors that make up EQ. The first two are "self-awareness" and "self-control." These two inward facing traits offer some of the first clues as to whether a business owner has the ability to develop a healthy culture.

Self-awareness is defined as "the ability to recognize and understand your moods, emotions and drives as well as their effect on others." (TTI 2008) A leader with high degrees of self-awareness is in touch with their feelings, they often appear calm, cool and collected. A leader with high self-awareness doesn't get surprised by stress and anxiety. This leader is aware of the things that bring stress on them and often stay ahead of them so as to not impact others.

Self-control is the "ability to control or redirect disruptive impulses and the propensity to think before acting." (TTI 2011) Being aware of your emotions and feelings are a healthy first step. Being able to control them before saying or doing the wrong thing is a different story altogether. Many high-driving business owners struggle with self-control. After all, it is often their driving, winner take all, attitude that helped make them successful and place them at the top of their organization.

But leaders with strong self-control tendencies know how to keep their emotions in check. They are great under duress because they don't have knee-jerk reactions to negative news. They are patient and positive, even when confronted with tough situations.

Highly effective business owners work to build high levels of EQ among their teams. And this starts by demonstrating it from the top. They also demonstrate the other factors of EQ: self-motivation, social awareness (empathy) and social skills.

When a leader builds an organization with people who have high levels of EQ, we know that influences a culture of empowerment. These employees who themselves exhibit high levels of EQ, are more engaged, perform at a higher level, and deliver quality products and services for the customers. These customers are highly satisfied and become loyal customers, offering great referrals and repeat business for your organization. We call this the EQ Value Chain. (TTI 2011)

3. Create highly, yet healthy, competitive environments.

Healthy competition is not punitive and is respective of all behavior styles. I worked for a High D business owner who was trying to increase the competition on our sales team. As the VP of business development I had a good handle on what my sales team wanted. Yes, money did motivate them to a degree. But more important to them were things like autonomy, creativity, and flexibility.

One team member enjoyed the autonomy I gave him to get creative with his customers and come up with truly innovative solutions. Another team member enjoyed the flexibility of time, as long as he was able to deliver on his expectations. Another enjoyed "farming" more than "hunting" and wasn't driven as much by big commissions as she was by taking care of a client and making sure they were satisfied with our services.

Each of these salespeople were successful in their own way. Each had their own unique driving forces. And while money was still the biggest carrot we had to offer, we could find other ways to motivate and encourage them.

By tailoring the incentives, I was able to motivate each team member according to their personal traits. And I was still able to maintain corporate level incentive programs based on volume, profit and other factors.

The important thing about this model is that we recognized that each team member had their own interests. There was very little competition between the team members. Each team member's competition was within themselves, to perform against their numbers. This helped us build a more collaborative environment, where they actually worked to support one another instead of against each other.

A one-size-fits-all program wasn't going to work in this organization. Furthermore, a winner takes all mentality would have destroyed morale on this team.

ADVICE FOR THE EMPLOYEE/COACH/ ADVISOR

This can be a tricky situation. Often a business owner has a specific idea of how they want their culture to be. In many situations, they might just want the highly competitive culture that they've built. But they may not be aware of some of the impacts it is having.

1. Ask them what they want.

I've asked this question to several business owners over the years, "What do you want?" They always say that they want a healthy culture. But many don't know how to build it. In their mind, a competitive environment may seem perfectly fine. Especially if that's matches their behavior profile.

When a business owner says they wants "healthy competition", I ask what they mean by that. Often I hear things like "they own their book of business," "they can make as much as they want to," or the one I shared earlier, "they work hard and play hard."

If they answer with these types of answers, I'll simply follow up with some questions about different styles. Nine times out of ten, this type of business owner will fall back on money as their one and only true motivator.

But money doesn't buy happiness, and it is not the only source of motivation for your team.

I encourage business owners to survey their team to find out what their motivators are. This can be done 1-on-1, through anonymous surveys, or by hiring someone like myself to come in and figure it out. Whatever the approach, learning the motivational factors for your employees is the first step toward building a competitive environment that takes everyone's interests into account.

2. Develop the EQ of your teams.

In an ideal world, the EQ of the organization starts from the top. But we don't always get to do it that way.

One of my clients had a leader with a very low EQ. Fortunately, her leadership team was composed of three leaders with high levels of EQ. They began working to improve the emotional health of their teams. In doing so, they isolated many of their team members from some of the destructive tendencies of the leader. But more importantly, they developed strong teamwork between their teams.

Evidence shows that when one team in an organization displays strong levels of EQ, it has a cascading influence on the teams they interact with. It's almost like a healthy virus being spread through the organization.

In the case of this organization, the teamwork and improvements exhibited by the teams themselves had an overall positive influence on the organization. They even led to higher levels of EQ being exhibited by the entire leadership team, including the owner.

3. Purge scarcity thinking.

"But we can't do that." How often do you hear that?

Whether it's "we've never done it that way," or "that will never work," I encounter this resistance all the time. Most leaders don't want to try something new because they fear the unknown.

Another cause of that fear is scarcity thinking. Scarcity thinking tells us that if we mess up, we may not recover from it. If I make a bad decision, I may lose my job. If the client doesn't like it, they'll go somewhere else. If I lose this client, I'll lose everything.

This type of thinking leads to a culture that is afraid to try new things, experiment and take risks. It's also indicative of an environment that is so focused on winning the immediate battle (the "finite game"), that we lose focus on the ultimate goal (the "infinite game"). (Sinek 2019)

WHEN IT STINKS

Earlier I mentioned the "work hard, play hard" organization I used to work for. I had a long run there, but the competitiveness eventually got to me.

One day I was having a 1-on-1 with the executive that led our department. He told me "John, you aren't competitive enough."

I disagreed with him and told him that my wife and golf partners would certainly say otherwise.

He explained, "When you come in here, every day you should be striving to prove that you are better than your peers around you. That you are the best at your level in the organization."

I responded by saying, "I thought my role was to come in every day and strive to do the best job for the *organization*, to work *with* my peers in order to achieve our department and company goals."

And how did this leader respond to my interpretation?

I'll never forget his response. He leaned toward me across his desk, and he said, "You are so naïve".

I knew that this organization's culture was headed into an abyss. I went home and told my wife that I didn't think I would be there much longer. And true to my instincts, about four months later I was offered a nice severance package to move on to other opportunities. And how did I feel being unemployed for the first time since college? I went home and slept like a baby. (And hopefully not an ugly one!)

You see, I had come to realize that an unhealthy culture is just that, unhealthy. And it was better for me to start a new stage in my life. So I did. I began to build my own baby, instead of being trapped within someone else's ugly one.

CTA – WHAT IS AN ORGANIZATIONAL HEALTH ASSESSMENT?

How is your organization performing today? Is it healthy? Are your leaders aligned with the Mission, Vision and Values of the organization?

Health Assessment

To put together an effective organizational development plan, we need to first establish a starting point. This assessment is customized to meet your needs. It includes components regarding strategic direction, meeting customer needs, internal processes, organizational capacity, and leadership.

The assessment will be an anonymous online instrument. It will be complemented with follow-up interviews with key personnel.

This assessment is the start of the planning process, which is a top-down process. We will then develop a plan to implement. Execution goes bottom-up. With this plan we will identify cause/effect breakdowns and go after the issues that need to be addressed first.

Financial Assessment

It is critical to also know how the company is performing against industry benchmarks. This assessment evaluates two years of financial data. The results are returned in plain English. We also provide a scorecard highlighting six areas of strengths and weaknesses. We compare 2 years of historical data against industry averages and benchmark assessments.

This analysis should be performed either after the books have closed for a fiscal year, or as a tool headed into strategic planning.

Watch video for more information.

CHAPTER 5

TWO EARS AND ONE MOUTH.

Several years ago, my dad was on a business trip to Atlanta. He was travelling with one of his co-workers, Ben. Ben wore hearing aids, and the sound of the airplane engines always bothered him. So, when he got on the plane, he would turn his hearing aids off so that he could rest.

On their return trip from Atlanta to Louisville, a short flight of just over an hour, Ben had turned his hearing aids off and was already resting at takeoff. But this trip was anything but normal. The plane had a mechanical issue that prevented it from getting to altitude. The passengers soon realized something was wrong as the plane did not climb to cruising altitude as normal. Instead, it flew at a level above the treetops, noticeably lower than normal.

There was a fair amount of commotion as passengers wondered what was going on. After several minutes of this, the pilot announced that they were having a mechanical issue and would be returning to the airport.

My dad tells how the nervousness was palpable in the cabin. And that many passengers were praying, some were crying, and all were worried.

The plane made a gentle turn, the pilot obviously cautious to maintain altitude and return safely to the airport. The plane returned safely to the ground, around 30 minutes after it initially took off. Everyone was safe and relieved.

When my dad saw his friend, who had slept through it all, he turned his hearing aids back on and said, "Wow, that was the fastest trip home I ever remember!"

HEARING AND LISTENING

Hearing and listening are two different things. Ben couldn't hear, and thus he was clueless about what was going on. Many leaders can *hear* fine, but they don't *listen*. And the results are similar.

I once worked with an entrepreneur who had a very unique approach to selling his product. He was extremely passionate, and often almost lost himself in the passion when he spoke to prospects.

I was working with him to help with his business development. My role was to get him front of industry leaders to sell his product. He had his sights set high, and my challenge was to get executives at some very large organizations to give him a listen.

One of the big targets was the entrepreneurial leader of a large corporation. This executive had a very impressive resume: Ivy League, MBA, JD. He was a very confident guy and did not waste time.

I was lucky enough to get him to sit down with me for coffee. I shared with him what we were trying to do and he was interested in hearing more. He expressed some doubts about the concept but was intrigued enough to give us an hour of his time.

We scheduled the meeting and set up all the details. The executive was going to come to our office for a presentation and demonstration. He was clear that he had one hour.

I spent time prepping Jim about our prospect's personality and expectations. I knew that my client had a tendency to talk over people and get too passionate about the product and lose track of both himself and his time. I asked him to talk no more than 10-15 minutes initially, gauge where the presentation is going, and then adapt. I also encouraged him to focus on the executive's organization and their unique needs, as I knew his ego would come into play.

Oh, the best of plans! When the meeting started our guest reminded us that he had exactly one hour. I introduced them and waited to see if my passionate entrepreneur would follow my guidance. He didn't.

He proceeded to jump right into his normal routine. He talked, and talked, and talked. Not once did he pause to ask any questions. I tried a few times to interject, but he talked right over me. Our guest was clearly exhausted and frustrated. He kept glancing at his watch.

Finally, the entrepreneur paused, 57 minutes after he started talking! The executive looked at his watch, jumped up and left. We never heard from him again. And the entrepreneur lost another opportunity because he did not know how to listen. Whether it was arrogance, nervousness, or cluelessness. The result was the same. And it was anything but successful.

Now this is an extreme situation, but I have seen it far too many times. Leaders who simply don't hear what people are trying to tell them. Sometimes this falls on the deliverer of the message, but more often it falls on the receiver. As leaders, we owe it to our team members to lead them in communications as well, and make sure we are receiving the information that we need in order to be successful.

WHY DO WE MAKE IT SO HARD?

I introduced the concept of cognitive biases in the first chapter. The most prevalent one, I believe, among business owners is confirmation bias. Confirmation bias is "the tendency to interpret new evidence as confirmation of one's existing beliefs or theories." (Oxford Dictionary)

But there are several others that come into play when it involves listening. For example, two that are easy to understand are optimism bias and pessimism bias. These biases are measured by the difference between the leader's expectations and the actual results that follow. If expectations are better than what actually happens, the bias is optimistic; if reality is better than expected, the bias is pessimistic. Whether we are overly optimistic or pessimistic, it has the potential to impact our ability to effectively comprehend what we are being told.

Affinity bias is another common bias. It states that we have an unconscious tendency to be favorable to people like us. So, if we realize that the person plays basketball, follows the same team, or graduated from the same school, that unconsciously gives us a positive feeling about that person, lending more credibility to their thoughts.

Priming bias can be quite destructive. It is the tendency by what someone is saying based on a preconceived idea. Often leaders are "prepped" for meetings. While often an effective method of steering the meeting in the right direction, it has the unexpected consequence of a leader going in with a preconceived notion and potentially not giving credibility to the person delivering the information.

Bottom line, cognitive biases create blind spots. This is when a cognitive bias impacts our judgment of others, while failing to see the impact of biases on one's own judgment.

We all deal with cognitive biases, and we can be completely unaware of them. I remember one time when this was presented to me like a punch to the face. I had been selected by my employer to attend a leadership program with the Center for Creative Leadership in San Diego, California.

I was excited to be part of this program. But I was nervous too. I heard it was quite intense and it was unnerving how much they got to the root of your behavioral issues. This particular program provided a two-day role-playing exercise where we ran a fictitious business and each had our own roles to play. I, for example, was the COO of a manufacturing company.

After the days of role-playing were done, we each had lengthy debriefs with the observers. They observed and videotaped us through two-way mirrors. (Yes, we knew it, and signed up for it!)

I was receiving my debrief and it was pointed out that I tended to override what someone says and put my own words in their mouth. I flat-out denied it. "I know I don't do that, I'm good at gathering info from others."

At that point she ran the videotape (yes, an actual videotape), and there it was. I was facilitating a discussion while standing at the white board. One of my team members gave me an idea, and I changed it to my own preferred words. It's like someone said the color was blue-green, but I preferred the word "aqua." They insisted that it was "blue-green." But I went ahead and wrote "aqua."

I was quite devastated to have this pointed out to me. But the most interesting part is that I still catch myself doing it to this day. While being self-aware of this bias, I still do it.

I realize now that everyone has their own set of preferred biases. The challenge is to learn how to recognize them and handle them when they surface. Interestingly, this is another example of self-awareness and self-control, the first two aspects of EQ.

WHAT'S A LEADER TO DO?

1. Implement the 80/20 rule for listening.

My wife was a middle school teacher for years. One thing I heard her say many times was "you have two ears and one mouth. Use them accordingly." The point she was making was that we should listen more than we talk. We would all be more successful if we practiced this.

But I actually take this concept even farther. I sometimes say we have "two ears, two eyes and one mouth." If we apply this ratio, receptor senses (eyes and ears) outnumber the mouth 4 to 1. This aligns with the 80/20 rule (or, the "Pareto Principle").

There are two points to apply from this metaphor. One, listening is not just an auditory activity. The most effective listeners use their eyes as much as their ears. They observe body language, facial expressions, gestures, posture, and more.

One of my clients is an outstanding example of this. She has an innate ability of detecting that something is going on in her team members' lives. She may not know exactly what is going on, but she knows something is. She becomes highly attune to their actions as well as their words. In most cases, she finds out later that there was a medical issue, family issue or other external factor impacting them.

Another application of this metaphor is the actual 80/20 ratio itself. I was taught years ago in some sales training that we should try to spend 80% of the time listening and only 20% of the time talking to a prospect.

For some, such as the entrepreneur I mentioned earlier, this may seem impossible. I used to have difficulty with it as well. After all, I like talking about myself. Now, when I prepare for a meeting, I often have a template of how I like the conversation to be structured. One of the reminders in the top corner of the page is simply 80/20. This is just a gentle reminder to me to always push the attention back at the person I am talking to.

2. Push the arrow.

I learned a technique that I employ if I find myself talking too much about myself. It's called "pushing the arrow." Imagine in your conversations that there is a piece of cardboard with an arrow on a spinner attached to it, much like you would see in an old board game. Except in this case, the arrow only goes two directions. It is either pointed toward you, or pointed toward the other person. Your goal in this game is to keep the arrow pointing in the direction of the other person. The concept is simple.

Now, imagine you have this arrow and it is placed on the table between the two of you. The arrow stays focused on the person on whom the attention is currently placed. So, if the other person is talking about their weekend, their children, or their business issues, the focus is on them. But when you are talking about your business or your interests, the arrow is pointing back at you.

Every time attention focuses on you, turn the arrow back to them, to their needs, to their interests. Make it your goal to not allow the arrow to stay on your side more than a few minutes at a time. Don't allow them to keep the focus on you.

Use open-ended questions. Open-ended questions cannot be answered with "yes" or "no" or any other one-word answer. Use questions that require them to dig deeper. Questions like "How did that make you feel?" will garner a much deeper answer than "That stinks, doesn't it?" Questions that make them come up with a list is another way of making them think. "What are your three biggest challenges right now?"

Active listening is another key to pushing the arrow. Lean forward, participate in the conversation. Acknowledge their points (without stealing the attention). And most importantly, respond actively with what they are saying.

Dig a little deeper with each question. Ask, "What's your biggest challenge with sales?" Then follow with, "What have you tried to do to fix it?" Followed by "What has worked for you?" Then "What is the most frustrating thing about this?"

Finally, use "reflection" techniques to repeat back and assess whether you have understood them correctly. This has the double-purpose of pushing the arrow back to them and allowing you to confirm that you have understood their point.

3. Listen slowly.

Another approach to good listening is "slow listening." Slow listening is a little harder concept to grasp. It means "listening for understanding." You must pay deep attention. This is "active listening on steroids." You may need to ask them to repeat and clarify info. Take your time and don't rush. Allow them to fully express themselves and give them plenty of time for follow-up and clarifications.

Slow listening goes beyond just listening with your ears. It involves listening with your entire body. Lean in. Focus on them. Make eye contact. Don't get distracted.

Watch for non-verbal clues. We use the term "body language." Well if it's a language, we should listen to it. In his book, *The Listening Life,* author Adam McHugh asks, "Why don't we use the phrase 'body listening'?" (McHugh 2015)

> "Hearing is an act of the senses, but listening is an act of the will."
> — **Adam S. McHugh, <u>The Listening Life</u>**

Slow listening takes energy. Staying focused on another person in a conversation takes emotional and psychological energy. It is not easy.

I have to admit that I struggle with this one. But one thing I do know is that when I come across someone who practices this, it absolutely empowers me. Consequently, I leave the conversation feeling appreciated, listened to, and important. When you do this for someone else, you leave them with these same feelings.

ADVICE FOR THE EMPLOYEE/COACH/ ADVISOR

1. Be curious.

One of the concepts that I learned in my training with FocalPoint is the importance of being "curious." Curious does not mean nosy. Curious means that you ask just enough of the right questions to allow the leader to discover the answers on their own.

As a coach, I want to ask open-ended, thought-provoking questions that will cause the business owner to think for themselves. Sometimes it feels uncomfortable. Often it feels repetitive. But by asking questions that get them to open up, you help them figure out what needs to happen.

By modeling this activity, we demonstrate the importance of listening. I find that when I model good behavior, it often is played back to me. When I get curious with them, they then get curious with me or with their team.

2. Interpret For Them.

Unfortunately, business owners and senior leaders often becomes disconnected from the ways and needs of the workforce. This can be an issue of socio-economic status, or it can be simply that their mind is focused on bigger picture items. Whatever the case, I find many leaders have become disconnected as a side-effect of their role and their success.

As their coach or advisor, you have the opportunity to "interpret" for them. Sometimes it is a matter of explaining what is happening on the front line.

I have found myself on the receiving end of this type of advice. I was leading a sales organization and I was confident in a particular product we were selling. I was hearing some "noise" from the operations side of the house, but I assumed it was just the typical complaints of learning something new. It wasn't until one of my team members took me into the field and showed me their issues that I understood what was going on.

I was listening, but the problem was discounting— or ignoring — what I was hearing. Fortunately, a team member took the time to interpret what happened and forced me to see the truth of what was going on.

3. Force understanding.

When interpreting doesn't work, sometimes you have to force the situation.

Have you ever watched *Undercover Boss*? The show demonstrates how a leader can easily become disconnected from what is going on in the field.

For example, the CEO of a company puts on a disguise and goes out and works with the front-line workers in their organization. They may work with a team in a store or a restaurant. Inevitably there are some issues that come about. They tend to fall into a couple of categories:

> • Poor performers who work against the values of the organization.

> • Those who are doing everything they can, but the odds are stacked against them. They may have been passed over for a promotion or they are a single parent

Those in the first category are dealt with appropriately. The latter are rescued from their situation by financial means or given opportunities that seemed impossible to them. These are the tear-jerker moments of the show.

The themes of each show are the same, but the responses are different. The point is that senior leadership is often so far removed from the front line that they do not understand the predicaments of daily life for the people who work for them. Senior-level management doesn't understand what a $10 increase to a copay on insurance means to the entry-level worker.

Going "undercover" might be extreme. Getting your senior-level executives to engage with and fully understand the concerns of their employees should be a goal.

CHANGE – GUARANTEED!

Here is one thing I promise. If you listen — really listen — to your team, you will see results.

I am not a traditional salesperson. I've never been trained in formal sales techniques, yet I have developed a good business for myself and once led a successful sales team. I attribute it to this one trait. I have learned how to listen.

I seldom put time limits on an initial sales conversation. If the prospect wants to talk for two hours, I will let them. I plan for this just in case. What I have found is that so few people are good at listening, that when someone actually does listen to them, they can't stop talking. Our conversation usually ends when they ask how we proceed.

And by the way, this is a good trait to bring home with you as well.

CTA – WHAT'S YOUR BUSINESS GROWTH SCORE?

Get a complete executive leadership report on you or one of the executives at your company... in just a few minutes.

You will receive an overall score out of 100 as well as individual scores for each of the five main areas of executive leadership. You will also receive a personalized report that breaks down your scores and gives you a plan of action for improvements. You get all of this at no cost. Zilch!

What did you want when you started in business? If you're like most executives, it would have included some of the following concepts:

- Having a clear vision.

- Leading with confidence.

- Achieving major goals.

- Working with a unified and motivated team.

- Communicating effectively with internal stakeholders.

- Managing their time effectively in their professional and personal lives.

If you happen to be like most executives, chances are your current reality doesn't quite reflect the visions you once had.

But it doesn't have to be this way!

GET YOUR FREE EXECUTIVE LEADERSHIP SCORE

CHAPTER 6

ROSE COLORED GLASSES. YOUR SALES PIPELINE PROBABLY ISN'T THAT GOOD.

"I'm going to call Jeremy!"

The owner of the company, my client, was excited to give an update to Jeremy, one of his major investors. Jeremy had put several million dollars into this startup.

"What are you going to tell him?" I asked.

"That we got the deal!" responded Stan.

One hour and five minutes earlier... the meeting was one I had organized between my client, the founder of a startup, and a decision maker in the government sector. There had been one meeting between my client and some members of this organization earlier in the year. The meeting was held in his small office overlooking the Ohio River.

My role was to help orchestrate business development meetings with key executives. I was excited to take this opportunity to the next level. We had heard rumors that there was going to be some movement with this prospect.

The meeting went well. While our guest did not divulge a lot of information, he gave us some clues as to their plans. He was part of a large government organization, with strict rules regarding vendor interaction and bidding processes. I had been in this game long enough to know not to expect too much.

When we got into more details around where their strategy was headed, he opened the door for my client's solution. We reminded him where the product fit into their strategy and how it could be the foundation for everything they wanted to do.

He agreed that this was possible. He also told us there would be a Request for Proposal ("RFP") coming out in first quarter of the following year (about six-nine months away), and that he would make sure to keep us informed regarding its timing.

The eager entrepreneur offered to provide additional specifications to help them put together the RFP. This is a common tactic, especially in the technology sector, where you can hope to get some proprietary specifications in the RFP, thus cutting out some or all competitors. The representative did not appear to be interested, despite several attempts. Our prospect was a consummate professional, and the rest of us in the room could tell that he was not going to cross any ethical lines.

The meeting ended professionally and friendly, and the representative went on his way. I followed my client back to his office. That's when the aforementioned interchange occurred.

"You got the deal?" I asked. "What conversation did I miss?"

"He practically told us we were going to get the deal. He even offered to use our specs." The intrepid entrepreneur replied.

I responded, telling him that I did not hear that, and that all I heard was that he promised to include us in an RFP.

I went on to say that giving Jeremy false hope could lead to problems down the road. If this does not play out as he expects, he will lose trust with his chief investor.

He agreed to weigh the probability of closure. So I asked him what probability he would give. "Ninety-five percent," he said.

Seeing the look on my face, he asked what percentage I would give. "Fifty percent at best," I responded. He was dumbfounded. The look on his face told me that he was incredulous. "My philosophy that any RFP is at best a coin flip, so I never give it more than 50 percent."

I continued to work for this client for a short time, but realized that his expectations were never in line with reality. I did speak with him a year or so later, and he confirmed that he did not win the bid. In fact, he didn't even bid on it because the RFP specifications did not line up with what he could deliver.

SALESPEOPLE AND SETTING EXPECTATIONS

While my formal training is not in sales, I have spent several years in sales roles. I have led the sales organization for a couple of technology companies, as well as being responsible for sales in my own business as well.

One thing I know is that salespeople are almost always "hedging their bets" whenever they report numbers. There are two competing factors that seem to go on whenever a salesperson is giving projections.

> 1. Every salesperson wants their leadership to believe that good business is coming. Therefore they often are overly optimistic on the likelihood of any deal coming through.

> 2. Every salesperson likes to have pleasant surprises to report, so they often don't want to give too much information too early. We call this "sandbagging."

I completely understand why they struggle with this internal battle. As the leader of a sales organization, I would have to defend our activity to our business owner on a regular basis. I would play through those same two scenarios each time I provided a report.

| If I was too optimistic, he would set high expectations for the month. He would assume deals to be closed before they were. He would then become disinterested when they actually came through (they were old news at this time). If they fell through, he would be aggravated because he had already mentally checked them off as done. | If I wasn't optimistic, he would be critical of our activity, stating that we weren't doing enough. As I would explain where we were working through the process with prospects, he would grow impatient. He believed we were chasing bad deals or not pushing our clients hard enough for closure |

Business owners and sales people often have a strange dichotomy. On one hand, the owner wants to believe everything is good (optimism bias). This is a great trait for a business owner. But a business owner must also be cautious at the right time, and not build unwarranted expectations, especially with investors, as in the previous story.

The business owner in this latter example, often took this to an extreme. Another area where this showed itself was in paying monthly commissions. Our salespeople were paid very well for their success. Our attitude was if they are successful, we would be successful. Their commissions were based on profits, not revenue. Which I believe is always a better approach when you can structure it this way.

In this particular industry, projects often took 60-120 days to complete. The lifespan of a deal would often span over six months. It might take one -two months (or often more) to close the deal. It then may take another two-three months to complete. Therefore, by the time it was completed and paid for, the project was very much "old news." Revenue would typically come in phases, primarily at the signing of the deal and after completion. It would take another 30 days or so to close out a project and determine its profitability.

By the time this was all said and done, we would have a monthly meeting to look at all jobs that were closed out. We'd determine the profitability and calculate the commission based on a sliding scale. Jobs with higher profitability would get a higher commission. Rewarding the salesperson for not missing any details and doing a great job of managing customer expectations.

The problem was the owner had already moved on from this project. It was old news to him at this time. Paying commissions was painful for him, as the money was already in the bank – and probably spent. It was the same two-headed monster from before, only now looking backward. If the profitability of the job was too high (which was good for everyone), he would be upset about how much he had to pay out in commission. If the profitability was too low, he would be upset about the team not meeting our expectations regarding profit margin.

ROSE COLORED GLASSES

The cause of most strife between owners and salespeople are generally based on expectations. The source of the problem is owners who have unrealistic expectations and the salespeople who help set them.

The challenge is in how you maintain balance in this world of setting expectations. One of the realities we must face is that many business owners and salespeople share similar traits. These include being decisive, outgoing, and optimistic. Let's face it, you don't typically take the risk of starting a business if you aren't optimistic, and certainly shouldn't if you aren't decisive.

When these two personalities get together, we often see them feed off each other. This trend leads us down the path of spiraling out of control into an overly optimistic view of what may happen. I refer to this as the "optimism spiral".

The "Optimism Spiral" occurs when two optimists feed on each other's energy and leave balance and reasoning behind. I've seen this happen most often with an optimistic business owner working hand-in-hand with an enthusiastic salesperson.

One of my clients has suffered with this for years. They are in the business of building new storefronts. Growth comes by getting in front of more clients to open up more storefronts. It's a numbers game. The more stores they have open, the more business they will see, and the more profits generated for its investors.

The challenge is that every year they go into planning with expectations to add as man as 15 more units. They put these projections together even though in their best year they may have opened 5 or 6.

Year after year they set expectations. Year after year they look back with disappointment and promise that next year will be better.

To get past this challenge, they need to bring a dose of reality to their projections. And if investor expectations are to hit a certain revenue target, perhaps they need to look at business model changes instead of just adding extra units onto an unrealistic projection.

WHAT'S A LEADER TO DO?

1. Implement a CRM or tracking system.

To be honest, I am not a fan of most customer relationship management (CRM) systems. It is not that I don't value what they do. It is just that I seldom find one that meets all my needs. But nevertheless, I have implemented and used them successfully in many situations.

Before implementing a CRM, you need to consider several things.

What is your true need of the system? Do you want it to track activity, to project sales volume, to provide estimating capability, or to enable project management?

If you spend some effort figuring out what you need, then you are more likely to find something that will meet those needs. Don't run out and buy the market leader just because everyone else is buying it. Each market has unique needs, and some products are better than others from market to market.

There are market leaders for IT services firms, online entities, healthcare sales, and so on. And there are others that are very generalized and accomplish specific tasks very well. Some automate email, some provide automation to scheduling and others integrate better with social media platforms.

Look at what you need, talk to people in your industry, and get plenty of demos. Ask lots of questions. This is a decision you will live with for several years. So do your due diligence. And find something that will help you manage expectations across your team.

2. Implement a system of checks and balances.

I mentioned earlier how salespeople and business owners are often wired very much alike. This leads to "optimism spiral" and a series of "attaboys." These in turn lead us into the abyss of unrealized returns.

I like to bring opposite minded thinkers into sales meetings. In particular, bringing in engineering, operations, or customer support can be eye-opening. This might not be a weekly activity, but at least once a month. It brings balance around the table as we discuss what the sales team is trying to accomplish.

To do this, you have to give these "opposite thinkers" permission to speak freely. Not rudely, but freely. I have found that we often adjusted our direction on some ideas after we considered the input from these other groups.

> This happens in all types of organizations, even non-profits. I serve on a non-profit board where I often am the person who brings the skeptical questions to the table. I do this not because I am wired that way, but because I notice an absence of these types of questioners at the table.

Many times we pressed on, even without the full buy-in from our counterparts. That is okay, as long as we are moving forward with a full disclosure and transparency of the potential risks as well as rewards. (Remember that sales and business owners tend to be risk-takers, while operations and engineering tend to be risk avoiders.)

These cross-functional discussions were almost always enlightening and usually led to better results. When you have buy-in with operations and support before the project begins, you have a much greater chance of success.

3. Execute and enforce accountability.

The back side of the sales process is holding salespeople (and the business owner) accountable for results. There are many approaches to this. Some fields, such as financial planning and insurance sales, have rigid models where poor performers are culled out before too much is invested in them.

Other industries, where sales are slower and relationship based, have longer lead times and it takes longer to determine the high performers from the rest.

I frequently use regular accountability meeting. I model these meetings after what I used to do in the IT world. We would have "scrums", which are short, typically standing-up, accountability meetings. In each meeting, each team member is asked three questions:

1. What have I accomplished?

2. What will I accomplish before the next meeting?

3. Where am I stuck?

There is no judgment or punishment in these meetings. Just simply the facts. There's no room for stories or excuses. We want to know what they've done and where they are going.

If you keep it simple, you focus on the accountability piece. And if you do that, you'll accomplish much more.

Salespeople always have a story. If they start telling a story around what they haven't done or why they haven't done it since last month, then politely move them on to the next task. If they only get to report on what they've accomplished, they find themselves working harder to accomplish something before the next meeting.

> When it comes to accountability there are only two types of answers: Stories and Results

ADVICE FOR THE EMPLOYEE/COACH/ ADVISOR

1. Train your salespeople on how to use a CRM.

Have I said it before that salespeople tend to be independent and optimistic? Of course, I have. And it's true. Consequently, the idea of implementing a system that tracks their activity might not be a popular decision. You will need to take some steps to overcome the resistance to implementing a CRM.

Salespeople need to be trained on the *use and the purpose* of a CRM. It should not be seen as a club to beat them with. Although, once a CRM is in place, it is much harder for an underperforming salesperson to hide.

There are a few common mistakes I see salespeople make in their use of a CRM.

First, I see them being overly optimistic on sales. Remember the business owner at the beginning of the chapter? Ninety-five percent probability is essentially a guarantee. I had a few rules for my salespeople in putting probabilities in the CRM:

> • Nothing is greater than 80% until a signature has been received

> • Nothing is less than 20%, we shouldn't be chasing anything that uncertain

> • There's no such thing at 50/50, 51/49, or 49/51 is okay, but don't give me a coin flip.

Second, they do not take advantage of the capabilities of the system. Depending upon what CRM you choose, it may streamline communication with clients, manage your inbox or help you calculate proposals. The independent streak that many salespeople have leads them to not take advantage of these tools. I have had to reprimand some of my salespeople to utilize the system the way it is intended.

Third, and closely related to the previous, is the tendency to simply use the CRM as a sophisticated spreadsheet. If that's all you are going to do, save the money and just use a spreadsheet.

2. Develop a safe, transparent culture of communication.

The cross-functional meetings that I mentioned before serve as checks and balances across the organization. These meetings will only be effective if open and honest communications are permitted.

The foundation of any healthy business relationship is trust. I have already written about the challenges of a hyper-competitive environment and how it impacts culture. If your environment has an unhealthy level of competition, I can guarantee that trust has flown out the window.

All too often, I have seen engineering and operations people shot down as being naysayers when it comes to sales opportunities. I have to plead guilty to sometimes being that person. Leadership needs to allow for a wide variety of opinions. Only in considering alternatives will you truly develop the best, balanced strategy to move ahead.

If your cross-functional participants are not openly pushing back or challenging the assumptions, you probably have a culture where they are afraid to speak up. So ask them. Encourage them to speak their mind. And remember what I said earlier, don't shoot the messenger.

3. Remove the business owner from the sales projection process.

This may not be possible, but it should be a goal. The business owner should respond to sales reporting, not be responsible for it.

When the business owner is responsible for sales reporting, their optimistic tendencies will dominate. They'll promise their investors that a big deal is "done." They'll spend money that hasn't been made yet. They'll commit to things before it's time.

When I set up the accountability meeting with engineering and operations, I did not include the business owner in the discussions. Why? There were several reasons. First, he would have intimidated people to not be open and honest about their opinions. Second, he would have squelched ideas that didn't match his viewpoint. And third, he would jump to conclusions and push ideas that were not ready to be promoted yet.

By the time we took information from those meetings to the business owner, the information had been vetted, the teams came to a conclusion, and we had realistic projections to put before the owner. While he was not always happy with the projections, I can assure you that we exceeded expectations far more than we fell short.

THE RESULTS ARE IN – REALISTIC EXPECTATIONS ARE ALWAYS MORE FUN

The company that implemented the CRM along with the checks and balances and accountability meetings is truly a model of how sales should work. Healthy skepticism, combined with tools and processes to keep everyone from their strongest tendencies helps make for a balanced and realistic model.

Many of the ugly baby scenarios I have seen in businesses are really not that ugly. The problem is that when you have unrealistic expectations, even good results can seem inferior. Proper expectations improve perceptions at every level.

When expectations are reasonable, the company performs better. Realistic expectations beget realistic budgets. Realistic budgets beget realistic staffing. Realistic staffing begets realistic results. And realistic results are just a lot more enjoyable.

CTA – WHAT'S YOUR BUSINESS GROWTH SCORE?

CHAPTER 7

YOU PUT THE "FUN" IN DYSFUNCTIONAL. LEADERSHIP THAT LIMITS GROWTH.

As a business owner, you have built an organization that is a living, breathing extension of what you began, and over the years, you have become less connected with day-to-day operations. Your business is likely run by others – people you trust, people you have hired and put in charge of taking care of your baby. But the reality is they are not you. And sometimes, they are not leading your organization the way you expected.

I performed an organizational assessment of a company that was experiencing some turmoil among its leadership. The owner had built the company from the ground up. They were very successful, a market leader. But there were issues, and he knew it. He was not exactly sure what was going on. He was just looking for feedback.

The organization assessment included interviews with the company's leaders, DISC assessments, sales assessments and even secret shopping them against their competitors. I shadowed some of the key team members and reviewed their sales and marketing strategies.

During the interview process, every leader told me the same thing. "This place is great, if it wasn't for Bobby." And, "We work great together, except for Bobby." Plus, "I love this place, but Bobby drives me crazy." And, "If we could only get Bobby in line..."

I couldn't wait for the chance to speak to Bobby! I'm not sure what I was expecting, but he was a pleasant surprise. He was a great guy – personable, engaging and talented. He knew his job and performed at an exceptional level.

But Bobby told me this, "No one here appreciates me. I feel like I'm on an island."

When I reviewed the DISC behavior results of the leadership team I discovered something very interesting. Everyone except Bobby fell in or near the C category. Some were naturally a D or an S, but their adapted scores all migrated toward the C quadrant. Everyone, that is, except Bobby. Bobby was a pure I.

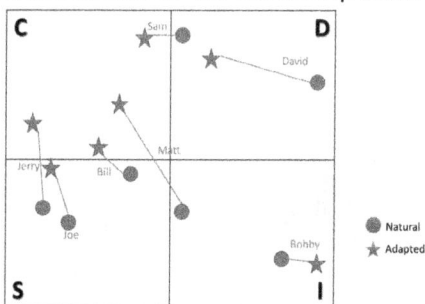

What did this mean? The C behavior type stands for Compliant. These are the rule followers. The C category is comprised of engineers, accountants, programmers and financial analysts. Cs make lists and stick to them. They love a good policy manual. You can never have enough data for a C. And you never want to vary from a policy if you are working with one.

The I behavior type is the exact opposite. The I is the influencer. This is the talker, the free thinker, the dreamer. To an I, a rule is more like a suggestion.

These two behavior types are constantly at odds. Have you ever worked in a company where sales was constantly battling with engineering or operations? This is why.

Bobby's role? He was their director of sales, and he was the top producer in the company. Over 90% of the sales were directly or indirectly his responsibility.

So the question comes, how can every single leader in the company think that Bobby needed to go? Simply put, their culture was one of precision and accuracy of every detail. Bobby simply wasn't wired that way. Neither was his sales team. So, when the rest of the organization demanded accuracy, Bobby and his team delivered results. Great results. Just without the level of accuracy and detail that the rest of the team would have preferred.

The problem had advanced far beyond petty feelings. They had implemented rules to punish those that did not follow their rules. A salesperson had a number of steps to follow in their paperwork. There were checkboxes and calculations, but no automation. Steps were expected to be followed. If a salesperson forgot to check a certain box, their commission would be decreased. The rule followers created more rules. And they were bound and determined to change the actions of their non-compliant sales team.

Did it have any effect? On performance, no. An Influencer is an Influencer, and they are unlikely to ever become a meticulously detailed Compliant. But on morale, you bet there was an impact. The sales team for this highly successful organization was beaten down. Morale was low. They were under-appreciated. And they awaited punishment at every turn.

The culture had taken a severe turn for the worse. A successful organization was headed toward a breakdown. A once beautiful baby had turned ugly. And the owner knew it.

Corporate shenanigans

I had an experience back in my IT days where another organization did not want to play nicely with our team. They had put together a project to do employee surveys. They utilized an external third party to put together the assessment tool. The only problem was that the company had no experience developing a tool for an organization our size.

The project was moving along and our testing demonstrated that the system performance would not be adequate. In fact, we were quite confident that the system would crash and wouldn't even function at a minimum level.

We expressed our concern to the executive who owned responsibility, but he was convinced that his people knew what they were doing.

After numerous attempts to thwart this and several emails to document our objection, we elevated it to our department leadership. When our leader took it to their executive, they were told to leave them alone, that they knew what they were doing.

The system was rolled out, it crashed, and everyone looked foolish. Leadership of the organizations got together and pointed fingers. The COO, who both of these departments reported to, was incensed. His own leadership had put personal egos ahead of the good of the organization. He was incredulous.

A SAD LIST

As I was thinking about this topic, I realized, sadly, I had far more examples about dysfunctional organizations and leaders than I thought. So here's my very sad, top ten list of the most dysfunctional leaders I have run across in my career:

> 10) The sales manager who cornered me on the first day on the job and asked me when my engineer was going to be finished with his task. In this company, everything was drama, and arguments were the norm. This sales manager was ready to pick a fight with me on day one. I was so new, I did not even know the engineer's name!

> 9) The organization that thought the best way to lead a reorganization was to eliminate every job and create a new org chart. Then every employee had to apply for positions. Those that did not get a position were let go. Some consultant made a lot of money selling them on that approach! It was one of the most demoralizing processes I have ever been through.

> 8) The director who called me almost ten times on one day while I was on vacation in Hawaii. He had heard rumors that a project I was leading was having difficulties. It was nothing critical, but he had to have an answer. And he had to have it at that moment.

> 7) The new manager that took over a team of senior leaders, only to tell us that he was smarter and more capable than any of us. He also made sure we knew that we were all expendable, so he did not want any of us to think we were "divas." This was one of my most short-lived tenures under any leader.

> 6) The director who required all of us to be on call 24/7 but refused to carry a pager or provide his home number (in the days before cell phones).

> 5) The manager who loved to demonstrate how much he worked. He would send emails between 2 AM and 5 AM, and was always quick to point out when you didn't respond promptly. I often wonder what happened to this leader. He must have flamed out.

> 4) The director who paged me while I was in the restroom because I wasn't working at my desk. Seriously. He saw that I wasn't at my desk and wanted to know where I was. My response to him is not one of my proudest moments.

3) The CEO and COO who argued with each other over the slightest of issues. The culture in this organization was to argue first and find solutions later. This was one of the most drama-filled organizations I ever worked with.

2) The CEO who hired a replacement for his sales director before telling his sales director he was firing him. While this didn't happen to me, I did have a similar experience once. And it was just as awkward.

1) The vp who told me I wasn't competitive enough. He cultivated a culture of unhealthy competition and was proud of it. This one will always rank at the top of this sad list.

When I look at all of these examples, from the company with Bobby, to the examples above, there is one common underlying problem. The absolute need for a sense of control. In every case, the manager, director or executive, needed to demonstrate their power. In almost every case, by the way, the leader was male. I have found there are often gender tendencies that happen with male leadership over other male team members, which opens up another topic that we will not explore here. (Suggested reading to dive deeper on this topic is *Gender Goggles: The Vision You Need to Get Promoted, Strengthen Relationships and Love Graciously*, by Jill Eaton)

WHAT'S A LEADER TO DO?

1. Understand your control issues.

Successful leaders understand that there is a careful balance in how much control you have and how much you delegate. The first step of a recovery program is admitting you have a problem. That comes with the addiction to control as well.

One of my clients had a problem with control. She controlled almost every administrative task in her organization. She balanced the books, processed payroll, and prepared invoices and client proposals. She did it all. As her company grew, her available time didn't. She found herself in a situation where she couldn't work *on* the business because she was too busy working *in* the business.

When I challenged her to delegate some of the tasks, she immediately raised her concern. She said, "I don't trust people." She had tried to delegate some of these tasks in the past, and it didn't go well. What does a typical control-oriented person do in that case? They hang on to their power as long as possible.

Once she realized her need to control everything, she found that it liberating to focus on higher value activities and grow her business.

Some of the leaders in that top ten list did eventually see the light as well. The one who called me on vacation eventually realized that he was working himself into a very unhealthy situation. Balance became his friend and he learned how to give up some of the control.

The VP who led the traumatic reorganization also realized she had made a huge mistake. She later apologized for the stress she laid on every member of the organization.

If you are having issues figuring out what to delegate, go back and reread chapter 3. In particular, look at your "areas of awesome" and see what you can eliminate.

2. Don't be distracted from the goal.

I shared some stories earlier from one of my employers. This was the company that had the hyper-competitive environment that encouraged managers to compete against each other.

In looking back, I realized one of the big problems I experienced there was that the organization leadership had taken their eyes off of the bigger goal. They were no longer focused on making the company successful. I have seen this play out in other organizations. The problem is when the focus is no longer in supporting the corporate goals, or even the department goals, it leaves room for people to focus on their own individual goals. And that almost never leads to success.

I have even seen individual goals disguised as organization goals. For example, a leader may present a goal as something for the whole organization to achieve, even though it is really something they, themselves, want to accomplish.

When the leadership becomes less focused on the purpose, vision, mission and values of the organization, they attend to their own personal needs and incentives. In doing this, they create a culture where no one truly understands what the real mission is.

> When the leadership becomes less focused on the purpose, vision, mission and values of the organization, they attend to their own personal needs and incentives.

I see this sometimes in organizations that like to post values and statements on their walls. My take on this has always been that if you have to write them on the walls, you probably aren't living them day to day.

When talking to clients about their values, I ask what are their "unwritten values". They first will deny any exist. But eventually, they will admit to a few. Some examples include never leaving work before the boss, always looking busy, and always being on call, even when you are not.

The real values of an organization are what its people live by every day. If these unwritten norms aren't aligned with the written values, then there will be a disconnect. And that is when you will likely see leadership inserting their personal goals into those of the whole organization.

3. Assess your organization's health

One of the most valuable moves you can make as a leader is to hire an outside entity to perform an organizational health assessment. If you want to demonstrate your vulnerability, hire a third party to do this, and give them full autonomy to conduct a thorough assessment.

When I conduct these assessments, they typically include the following:

- Individual assessments of leaders to identify behaviors, motivators and emotional intelligence

- Interviews with key leaders and staff

- Omni-directional surveys with employees, executives, clients and vendors

- Shadowing key team members to understand their role

- Mystery shopping of retail and service providers

This is one of the most vulnerable tasks of a leader. By allowing an outside entity to perform a thorough assessment, you are allowing someone to come in and peek around every corner. It reminds me a little of that leadership program I participated in where I was being observed behind a two-way mirror.

On a different note, one of the questions I often get asked is how to deliver bad news to the CEO. The answer, besides "very carefully", is to present information as facts. Also, present it to the leadership team together with the CEO. If there are negative comments, it is far better for it to be shared with them as a team. That way they can review and respond as a team.

But if there is anything highly "flammable," I will give the CEO a heads up. Remember, no one likes to be told their baby is ugly.

ADVICE FOR THE EMPLOYEE/COACH/ ADVISOR

1. Don't add fuel to the fire.

As an advisor to the business owner, be careful not to use this to pursue your personal agenda. On one occasion, a leader in the organization saw the disarray and deteriorating culture as an opportunity to advance their own career.

In this situation, the person was in a role where she was able to review performance of teams and recommend direction for the future. She used her position and influence as a way to attempt to remove competition for leadership positions she desired.

It is better to support the good of the whole organization than to worry about self-promotion. Opportunities to grow almost always come to those who strive to lead the organization to success.

Motives are not easily hidden. In this situation, her motives were quickly discovered. She did not survive in her role for long.

2. Expose control issues as power grabs

When you see control issues appear, do not allow them to fester. I remember a client on a project who was trying to establish his own power in the organization. He used a small project to establish his leverage and attempt to raise his profile.

In a project debrief, he went on the record with our Project Management Office (PMO) with his review of the project. The project manager started the review with a few questions.

She asked, "What are some of the things that went well with the project?"

His response was something like "The project was not completed on time."

The project manager said, "Let's focus on some of the good points, and then we'll look at what could have gone better."

He then said something like "We did not get all of the features we wanted."

And so it continued. He was the client manager on the project, and he shared in its success. The project was a success, but he could not bring himself to complement anything about the project or the team.

The problem with this client was simple. He wanted to demonstrate his power and control over the situation, and he became very frustrated when his complaints were just seen as "noise."

His attitude and approach were quickly noticed by all that worked with him. His stature in the organization did not grow like he expected.

3. Work hard on the culture.

Culture is hard. Let me say it again. Culture is hard.

Culture happens by accident without even trying. But, establishing the culture you *want*. That's hard.

CULTURE IS HARD

So, work hard at culture!

As a leader, advisor or coach to the CEO, your role is to help them strategize how to establish the desired culture. The challenge in establishing a culture is that it actually means changing the existing culture. Think about this. A culture is established almost as quickly as the organization is established. Norms, hierarchies, unwritten rules, and alliances appear within days if not moments of an organization's founding. To establish a culture, then, means to change the culture that has already been established.

We often use the word "change management". I would like to change this phrase and replace it with "change leadership". I believe this is a much more effective way of driving change in an organization.

When I work with a leader to establish change, we utilize Gleicher's Formula for Change. This model, which is taught as a mathematical formula, provides a way to assess the key components to overcome barriers of change. The formula was created by David Gleicher while he was working at Arthur D. Little in the 1960s, and it was later revised by Kathie Dannemiller in the 1980s. (Dannemiller 1992)

Dannemiller's version of the formula is expressed as follows:

$$D \times V \times F > R$$

R in this formula refers to the resistance to change. For any change to be implemented, you must overcome the resistance that the organization puts up. Do you think there is resistance when leaders try to change culture? You bet there is.

The equation is expressed as an inequality (the ">" tells us this). For a change to be successful, the product of the items on the left must be greater than the resistance in the organization.

The three variables on the left are:

> D = Dissatisfaction. This is a measure of the amount of dissatisfaction with the current state.

> V = Vision. This is the clarity of vision that the leader can paint of the future.

> F = First Steps. This is measured as the ease of taking the first step toward the change.

These three variables are multiplied to come up with the product. If the product of this formula is greater than the resistance, then the change has a high probability of success; however, if any of the three factors are ignored, non-existent or very small, then the impact to the formula is profound. Just as in mathematics, if any of the three items are zero, the product of the three is zero. Therefore, we must address all three as a part of our change leadership.

In the previous chapter I talked about an organization that successfully implemented a CRM system. We had attempted and tried it several times, but were unsuccessful. We finally were able to successfully implement the change. But it was a culture issue as much as it was a technical one.

How so?

> • People were dissatisfied (D). Commissions were being impacted due to lack of communication early in the project. Engineering was being brought into conversations too late, causing technical problems. Profits were down, frustrating the owners. Eventually the level of dissatisfaction reached a level where people were willing to change and make the investment in the system.

> • There was a clear vision (V). A better solution was found, that closely mirrored the work flows already in place. Demos were relevant, and a trial period was provided so we could see how it might work. These steps provided clarity around what the future could look like.

> • The first steps were simple (F). We invested in enough support to provide adequate training, build templates and our leaders invested heavily in their time to make sure the

implementation went smoothly. Therefore, the first steps were relatively painless.

Without realizing, we had utilized Gleicher's formula and successfully implemented a tremendous amount of cultural change in an established organization that had previously refused to take these steps.

BRING FUN BACK

While many organizations that talk about having fun are dysfunctional, it is possible to work in an effective organization with a healthy, supportive culture and have fun.

CTA – READER CONTRIBUTION SEGMENT – SHARE YOUR "BAD BOSS STORY"

I've had some crazy bosses, that's for sure. I shared some of the most outlandish examples of poor leadership that I could remember. Share your stories. Maybe they'll make it in a future book.

Online submission form

CHAPTER 8

IMPOSTER SYNDROME IS REAL – AND IT CAN BE HARMFUL TO YOUR TEAM.

"Don't refer to me as that," my client said, after I had introduced her to someone as the CEO of her company.

When we were able to debrief later, I asked her why she said that. She gave me several reasons for why she shouldn't be considered a CEO.

- CEOs are in big companies, not a small one like hers (she had about 10 employees).

- I don't feel like a CEO.

- I don't want to be a CEO.

- That's just not me.

- I feel like a fraud.

That last one is the kicker isn't it? When a leader doesn't believe they deserve to be in the position they are in, they believe themselves to be a "fraud," or an "imposter." Imposter syndrome is a psychological state in which a person doubts their talents, skills, ability, position, or power. Even when their status has been earned with countless examples of personal and professional success, they feel as a "fraud" in their current role.

Research suggestions imposter syndrome is predominantly an issue with women, but anyone can experience it. I, for one, can attest to that.

While it can be part of larger psychological issues, the most common types of imposter syndrome occur in every day common ways and leads to stress and anxiety. I find almost every business owner secretly, and sometimes not-so-secretly, struggle with it from time to time.

(And yes, this author has had his own struggles with this as a business owner, corporate executive and church leader. Not to mention book author – who am I to think anyone would read my book? Thanks, by the way.)

> I recently was working with a female executive coaching client who was up for a big promotion at a large international manufacturing firm. From our very first session, she voiced her doubts as to whether she was deserving of such a big job. She was vulnerable from the start, unlike my male clients who usually won't be so until after we have established a level of trust.

Imposter Syndrome is another example of cognitive bias. It is similar in nature to the bias called the Dunning-Kruger effect. This bias states "that people, at all performance levels, are equally poor at estimating their relative performance." Those with low to average ability tend to overestimate their ability, while those with above-average ability tend to underestimate their own. (Kruger and Dunning 1999)

WHEN YOU SEE IT IN YOUR LEADER

The topic of this chapter is unique in that it is not as much an organizational issue as much as it is an individual one. However, this bias, which can be exhibited at any level in the organization, is most dangerous in the mind of its leaders. If left unchecked, your team members may lose confidence in you, and consequently, the organization as a whole.

When the organization's leader struggles with imposter syndrome, they come off sounding like the old comedian Rodney Dangerfield, whose tagline was "I get no respect." Self-deprecating humor can be an effective method of building rapport and demonstrating a level of transparency and authenticity. However, if taken to an extreme, it just reminds you of a worn-out comedy routine.

When people overestimate their abilities, it leads to similar results. Overly optimistic goals and unrealistic expectations are the norm in this situation. As I shared in the previous chapter, many of the salespeople I have worked with have struggled with this. CEOs who rose from the ranks of salespeople create unique challenges. I have worked with several who rose from the ranks of salesperson, or more likely, were the original salesperson of the organization. They obviously were good at what they did, since they are now the CEO. But when duties expand and they are not totally dedicated to sales, their effectiveness may wane. As results falter, confidence in the leader follows. Over time, staff loses confidence because the leader is always promising better days with better results, but they never come.

Individuals with a combination of high D and high I scores (high in Dominance, how you make decisions, and high in Influence, how you interact with others) struggle with being perceived as glib. In fact, my own assessment stated that fact. I am combination of a high D and high I, and the assessment results show that under pressure, people may see me as "glib." It's a word that I don't use a lot, so, of course, I googled it. What I read was that while I was fluent and voluble, I also could come off as insecure and shallow. Ouch!

This can become dangerous for a leader. Appear too weak and vulnerable, and your team becomes uncertain about your ability to take the organization where it needs to go. If you come off as glib, they see you as lightweight, overconfident, and unable to achieve what you say you will do.

CONFIDENT, BUT NOT ARROGANT

Business owners need to walk the fine line between confidence and humility. We want our leaders to be confident. This is a mindset issue. Having a confident mindset — confidence in your beliefs and actions —leads to success. Some traits of confident leaders are:

- They take risks that propel their company forward.

- They invest in others without fear or pride.

- They surround themselves with others that are equally as strong, or stronger than they are.

Often when a leader lacks confidence they operate out of a fear mindset. This fear leads to actions that are the opposite of those listed above. It's a scarcity mentality.

While we want leaders to display confidence, we do not like leaders that are arrogant. I mentioned some toxic leaders I have worked for in the past in the previous chapter. One of those mentioned took over a team of senior IT professionals. He had previously led in different functions, where the leader had to be much more hands-on, and directive in their style. This fit his behavior profile. However, when he took over a team of seasoned professionals, he found himself in a situation where he needed to learn how to coach instead of tell. It was less about him solving problems and more about inspiring others to action. This did not fit his behavior profile, and created a toxic situation. His tenure in that role did not last long.

AUTHENTIC, BUT NOT WEAK

We love our authentic leaders. In many ways, this is a 21st century phenomenon. We will analyze the cause of this for decades.

But I believe our concept of leadership has in and of itself evolved. In many ways, it seems to be an outgrowth of servant leadership, a 20th century concept that has taken almost a half-century to take root.

Several of my executive clients are striving to figure out how to be an authentic leader. Here are a few scenarios:

- The CEO who has lost passion about the business. It's showing on his face every day. How does he rekindle the energy?

- The business owner who had an employee embezzle money from the company. How transparent should – or can – he be with his team?

- The business owner who had taken the eye off the details and allowed the company to sink into a financial crisis. Telling the truth may cause stress or even an exodus of key personnel.

- A client coming to the realization that their company performance is not what it needs to be, even while they have been the chief champion and cheerleader of its cause.

Finding the right time, place and tone to share is a critical part. If a leader has not been transparent, it is a huge and difficult step to suddenly share everything (and maybe not wise). Balance and forethought need to come into play as well.

While we want our leaders to be authentic, we do not want them to appear weak. One of the most common questions I get from my executive clients is, "How can I be more of a transparent servant leader, without being a pushover?"

I believe this question is rooted in a misconception in what servant leadership is all about. Being authentic and transparent, both highly desirable traits of the modern leader, do not require you to be weak. In fact, it is just the opposite. These traits require courageous leaders that are not focused on themselves, but instead invest in those around them.

When we have the courage to share our weaknesses, it strengthens us in the eyes of our team. A leader who admits the struggles they are facing, will largely garner the support of their team. Admitting your baby is ugly is not easy, but it is a start for building back the trust and support of your team.

WHAT'S A LEADER TO DO?

A leader dealing with imposter syndrome can be a real problem for a company. Problems range from appearing weak and losing trust and confidence of your team, to becoming so obsessed with your own problems that you lose touch with what is going on in your company.

The bottom line, in my opinion, is for the leader to quit focusing so much on themselves and turn their focus outward.

1. Practice gratitudes and affirmations each morning.

These concepts have long been a staple of coaching and personal performance. While two distinct concepts, I package them together because they require a mindset change. While they each stand on their own, I find it more effective for me to practice them together.

First, get in the habit of giving gratitude each morning. There's an old church hymn written by Johnson Oatman that goes "*Count your blessings, name them one by one*". The method I use for doing this is to articulate three things that I am thankful for. I recommend writing them down into a journal. And if it's your practice, incorporate them into a prayer.

I also don't repeat any of my gratitudes for at least 21 days. This might not seem hard, but I promise that it is a challenge. The first week is easy, "I'm thankful for my wife, for my kids, for my grandson, for my clients, for my home, for my ..." But you start having to think harder around day seven or so. By the time day 15 rolls around, you are really having to dig deep.

Second, I follow my gratitudes with affirmations. Author Brian Tracy encourages us to use affirmations that are composed of the "three P's." These are personal, present tense, and positive. Personal affirmations may range from something as simple as "I like myself" to "I am good at my job." Present tense means to state it as if it is already happening, such as "I am a successful leader." Finally, positive means to state things in the positive sense. Don't say "I am not going to lose this account." Say, "I closed the big deal today." It's easy to use negative words, but our minds tend to focus on them, so avoid them at the start your day. (Tracy n.d.)

2. Adopt a servant leader mindset.

The term servant leadership was coined by Robert Greenleaf in an essay in 1970, but it has roots going back many centuries.

As already discussed, the concept of servant leadership is in sync with the ideas of balance between confidence and authenticity. The concept of servant leadership is often misunderstood.

Servant leadership takes guts. It takes a huge heart. It requires a leader to put their entire team on their shoulders. Servant leaders are great listeners and are empathetic, this takes courage to not be self-centered. Servant leaders also have the ability to visualize, inspire and encourage their teams. They realize that they cannot achieve greatness alone. Therefore they strive to raise the performance of their team.

Greenleaf postulated that a servant leader focuses on the word "serve" over the word "lead." He came to two conclusions:

- I serve because I am the leader

- I am the leader because I serve

Putting service first, changes your entire perspective as a leader. But Greenleaf's work was highly theoretical and lacked specificity; therefore, many others added to his work and deepen our understand.

One of the most influential pieces of work was Larry Spears' "Ten Characteristics of a Servant Leader." (Spears 1998) The ten characteristics are as follows:

1. Listening – Communication is a two-way process, and many leaders are very good at doing the talking and less so at listening (see chapter 5). Effective servant leaders can listen intently and respectfully and then act on the information they receive. Servant leaders also make it easy and comfortable for those closest to them to provide honest feedback.

2. Empathy – You should be able to deeply understand and empathize with others, especially those you work closely with. It is important to recognize and accept people for their uniqueness and understand their point of view. This characteristic is essentially an extension of listening. You cannot be empathetic with people until you are attentive to them.

3. Healing – Do you care about your people? I mean, really care? This isn't about physical healing, but instead is about healing the inner person. If listening and showing empathy is a start. Helping people heal is the next logical step in a relationship. How do you react when you find out one of your team members is struggling with a personal problem?

4. Awareness – Effective leaders have a wider and deeper awareness of themselves and those around them. These foundational elements of emotional intelligence come into play here. Leaders who are self-aware have a better understanding of the impact of power, ethics and values. They make decisions from a more holistic perspective.

5. Persuasion – Servant leaders persuade instead of command. They rely largely on persuasion and cooperation to get things done, rather than through traditional methods of authority and delegation.

6. Conceptualization – Servant leaders have the ability to look at a problem from a perspective of conceptualization. This means they step back from day-to-day reality and can envision a bigger picture with a better reality. This idea is best demonstrated in Martin Luther King's "I Have a Dream" speech.

7. Foresight – Foresight is a characteristic which enables servant leaders to understand lessons from the past, the realities of the present, and the consequences of their decisions. Instinct and intuition come into play, but should be balanced with facts, data and input from trusted sources.

8. Stewardship – This characteristic is about responsibility and accountability. Servant leaders take responsibility for their actions as well as those of their team. Furthermore, Greenleaf's view was that leaders should play a significant role in establishing their institution in trust for the greater good of society.

9. Commitment to the growth of people – Servant leaders are committed to the personal and professional growth of

their people. They believe that people have an intrinsic value beyond just the work they do. Equipping and mentoring their team members is a key function of a servant leader.

10.   Building community – Servant leaders view their organization as more than just a "business." They strive to build a sense of community within their organizations. This can be difficult. Effective leaders encourage people to interact across artificial boundaries, develop relationships and support each other beyond the day-to-day tasks of the job.

Becoming a servant leader is not an easy task. For some it comes more naturally. Others fall back into the old habits of traditional command and control. Making these changes will take time. If your organization does not have a culture of servant leadership, it may create havoc. You may find some of your internal leaders are not on board. Organizational changes may be required in order to make it happen.

ADVICE FOR THE EMPLOYEE/COACH/ ADVISOR

If you work with a business owner or leader who struggles with imposter syndrome, you might be inclined to try and support them in this belief. For example, if a leader is being authentic and vulnerable and expresses doubts of their leadership, you may have a tendency, unintentionally, to support those beliefs. This can be by the most innocent of acts such as nodding your head or stating that you understand why they feel this way.

The best thing you can do for your leader is to help build their confidence through providing them with the gratitudes and affirmations that I wrote

Shortly before this book went to press, I was attending our international convention for members of the FocalPoint Coaching team. At our annual banquet, several awards are given out. One of the top awards is the Campbell Fraser Award for Coaching Excellence. In our business, this is a very prestigious award, given to the coach that truly embraces and demonstrates the "heart of a coach". This author was stunned to be named the recipient of this year's award. How did I feel? Elated for a few weeks. Then, I began to wonder and doubt. Why do they think I deserve this? I asked myself. Then I remembered this topic. Any of us can fall victim to Imposter Syndrome. It can happen at any time.

about in the previous section. Many people do not see these in themselves. By being a source of encouragement to them, you will equip them to be the leader they need to be.

For example, I mentioned that I sometimes struggle with imposter syndrome as well. One thing that I have done is saved a number of the emails, voice mails and other messages I have received from grateful clients, former team members and business partners. I sometimes re-read them just to remind myself of the positive influence I have had on others.

CONFIDENCE AND AUTHENTICITY WILL BUILD THE CULTURE YOU WANT

Get out of your own way, trust in yourself and practice these new habits. If you do, you will begin to build a new culture in your organization. It will take time. Patience is key. It may take some big changes. For some team members, it may not work. Some employees require a different style of leader. Some managers cannot lead in any other way. But if you want to quit "faking it," and purge imposter syndrome from your mind. Turn your focus on others, and it will take care of itself.

CTA – WHAT'S YOUR BUSINESS GROWTH SCORE?

Talk about perceptions. May have a video where I share the discoveries from my own DISC assessment.

CHAPTER 9

SHE'S JUST NOT THAT INTO YOU – WHEN YOUR BUSINESS ISN'T WORTH WHAT IT'S WORTH TO YOU.

I was once a member of a strategic collaborative of IT service providers from around the country. We met quarterly to learn from industry experts, share ideas, and improve our leadership and organizational capacity. At one of these events I was talking to the president of the organization. I mentioned how the owner of the company I represented was privately seeking interest in potentially selling his business. The president of the organization looked at me and said, "Every one of these business owners is secretly seeking out potential buyers, so it's not really a secret." We laughed at that and I asked why more acquisitions didn't take place. He said, "Because every owner thinks his business is worth more than it is. And every buyer is looking for a bargain."

It reminds me of the boat owner I knew who had a "For Sale" sign in his boat window. "Are you selling your boat?" I asked, slightly perplexed. He said, "Every boat is for sale, you just have to find the right buyer at the right time, and at the right price."

I guess many business owners are like the latter. If the right offer comes along, they will gladly walk away and do something else.

However, selling a business is not an easy decision for most business owners. This is especially true for founders. In this case they gave birth, they nurtured, they suffered through the awkward teen-age years, and they finally have a real grown-up business. Walking away from it is not an easy thing to do.

Selling a business has a number of unique aspects to it. If you've never sold a business, there may be some surprises in the process as you work through it. I've been involved with several transactions. Some have gone very smoothly, and others not so much. There is a great deal of planning and thought that should go into it before you make the decision.

LIKE SELLING A HOUSE

There are some similarities to selling a house. First, you don't decide to sell a house on a whim. You usually have thought about it for a while. Second, the price can vary greatly depending upon the perceived value and the desires and needs of those involved on both sides of the transaction. Finally, many things beyond the basic facts can come into play to affect the final price.

Similarly, when selling a house you typically don't just put it on the market and sell it "as is." I know some do, especially in the flipping business. Most sellers will make sure to take care of any cosmetic details, clean up messes, and stage the house to be shown in its best light.

In selling a business, the owner will need to do similar things. Cosmetically, are there any blemishes to be found? These could be with products, social media reviews, property issues or even team culture. To maximize value, the business owner may want to address as much of this as they can.

TIMING IS EVERYTHING

I recommend clients plan on an 18-month path toward selling their business because most "cosmetic" issues find their way to the profit and loss statement (P&L). You need to demonstrate that you have a track record of optimum performance before putting the business on the market.

Consider one of my clients who first talked to me about selling their business a few years ago. He attended one of my exit-planning workshops. I gave him this same recommendation, that he should plan on an 18-month lead time before putting it on the market. About 18 months later he came to me and told me he was "ready to sell." And by that, he meant that he was ready at that very moment.

We proceeded to look at his business and conduct an organizational review, looking at several areas beyond financial reporting.

Financial reporting is the key to determining business value. We look at the P&L, balance sheet, and other key factors in putting together a business valuation. We also look at factors such as how much money the current owner is taking out of the business and how much they are investing back in. In the real estate comparison, this is the essential equivalent to knowing the size, number of rooms, and condition of the property to look at "comps", or comparative values to other homes with similar traits that have sold in the area.

In our organization assessment, however, we dig deeper. We look at other areas of interest to include the history of the organization, the quality of its customer base, marketing and name recognition, and the impact of its leader leaving.

With this client we discovered that they had not raised prices in a very long time. In fact, labor prices had remained the same for over a decade! Furthermore, we established that price was not a key concern to the owner as his customers were "sticky" and were primarily repeat business. His reputation spread by word of mouth, so he had a fantastic reputation and did not have to invest much in marketing and branding.

When we came back with a business valuation, the owner was not happy with the numbers we shared. We were about $200,000 or so less than what he believed the business was worth.

But here is what is interesting. If they had been using standard industry pricing, the increase in revenue from labor would drive approximately $100,000 to the bottom line. At a multiple of somewhere just over 2.2, it would have increased his business valuation by some $250,000!

If the owner had engaged with us 18 months earlier, he would have raised his labor prices at that time. He would then have the established higher profit margins and his business would have been valued at what he was hoping for.

Unfortunately for this owner, he still needs to wait about 18 months so that he can establish the value for his business.

UNDERSTANDING YOUR VALUE

Another business owner I was working with had a very inflated view of what his business was worth. Perhaps one reason is that he had overpaid when he purchased it. He was under the misguided impression that revenue drives valuation, instead of profits.

He was interested in selling his business and we roughed out what it may be worth. I recommend bringing in a business broker to do this type of activity. But knowing what I know about the business, I could give a rough number. He was off by a factor of 10! That is because, in his mind, a business bringing in $20 million in revenue ought to be worth at least $20 million. But when profits (or more specific, EBITDA, earnings before interest, taxes, depreciation, and amortization) was less than one million, the value was really closer to $2 million.

Yes, here's another ugly baby moment. And nothing tells a business owner that his baby is ugly more than making an offer one-tenth of what they think it's worth! It is a very frustrating moment for a business owner.

> EBITDA, or Earnings Before Interest, Taxes, Depreciation, and Amortization, is a preferred measure of an organization's overall financial performance. Most prefer it over net income as a better starting point for calculating a company's value.
>
> EBITDA = E + I + T + D + A
>
> E = Earnings (Net Income)
>
> I = Interest
>
> T = Taxes
>
> D = Depreciation
>
> A = Amortization

But this misunderstanding is not that uncommon. I recently had another client reach out to me with the same point of confusion. Someone had floated an offer for her business, apparently based on revenue, not EBITDA. Upon further research, this deal did not go through.

WHAT'S A LEADER TO DO?

1. Conduct an exit-planning discovery process.

Before jumping in and putting your business on the market, I recommend the business owner go through a discovery process to prepare for their exit strategy. This discovery process has three aspects: A business valuation, a personal financial analysis and an organizational health assessment.

The business valuation is a fairly straightforward process. Some accountants provide this service. I prefer to use a business broker because they have a better handle on industry trends and can be great sources of advice for you.

A business broker will remove owner-specific expenses such as their income, benefits and other discretionary expenses. It's important to properly account for any personal expenses paid by your company so that you can properly remove them from this calculation. I know some business owners like to cover personal expenses with their business in order to save on taxes. But this can be very short-sighted. For every dollar in savings you may save $0.30 on taxes, but reduce your business valuation by over $2.

Personal financial analysis is often overlooked. What does the business owner plan to do next? Are they planning on retiring, starting a new business, buying a beach house, or working at the local hardware store? I bring in a certified financial planner to analyze the owner's financial position and determine how much they will need to get out of the business in order to achieve their goals.

Finally, I recommend conducting an organizational assessment to assess many of the other intrinsic elements of the valuation. In this assessment we look at organization issues such as the team, culture, leadership and the viability of the organization once the owner is gone. We examine items like brand reputation, opportunities for growth, needed investment and legal issues.

Once we have completed these steps, we put together a prioritized action plan. This may include suggestions (e.g., increase labor rates) or concerns (e.g., leadership void or a gap in financial goals).

At this point the business owner has a decision to make. In some cases, they know that they cannot move forward with their plans. However, if they want to move forward, we would move into the preparation phase.

DISCOVER	PREPARE	EXECUTE

Business Valuation

Assess Personal Finances → Prioritized Action Plan ◇ Build Exit Team → Financial Planning / Business Improvements → SELL

Assess Company Health

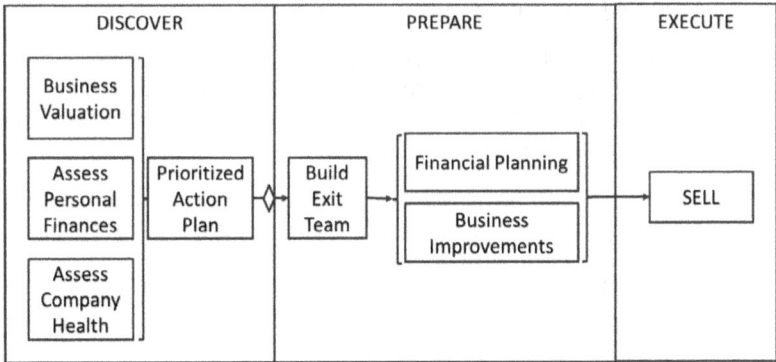

2. Don't decide alone.

This is a big decision for an owner. After completing the discovery phase, the business owner will have a lot to consider. The decision may be more than financial.

One client had been considering selling his business for several years. Once we completed the organizational health assessment he realized that he had allowed a toxic leadership culture to develop. We also showed where he needed to make a significant investment in technology, which was outside his comfort zone. Between the very fair offer he was offered, and the organizational issues we presented to him, he decided it was time to sell and head into retirement.

Every business owner should have a team of advisors to help them on this decision. Members of this team include:

- Business coach or strategic advisor
- Business broker
- Financial planner
- Certified public accountant
- Attorney
- Banker

There may be others, including a personal mentor, co-founder, investors, industry expert, and more.

This team should review the prioritized action plan from the discovery phase. The team recommends to the business owner what next steps should be. As the previous chart indicates, the team should transition into two tasks, conducting financial planning and making business improvements.

Additionally, the team needs to determine the timeline for taking the business to market. Our recommendation is to start with an 18-month assumption if you need to show financial improvements. In some cases, finances may not be the issue. In those cases, the timeline may be shorter. In other situations, it may take a couple of years to implement the necessary changes, such that the timeline becomes much longer.

2. Find a strategic buyer.

There are three types of buyers: opportunistic, entrepreneurial, and strategic.

An opportunistic buyer is one who is looking for a good deal. If you rush to market without doing your homework and preparing your business, this is who you are likely to find. Opportunistic buyers are not going to pay top dollar. They are like the house flipper looking for an off-market opportunity.

Entrepreneurial buyers are a better find. Like the former, they are looking for a good deal. But they recognize that they are going to have to pay fair market value for a good business. Their goal is to come in and work their magic to take your company to the next level. This may be an investor who believes they can bring better technology to your solution, improve your sales or operational processes, or bring a higher level of leadership to the team.

Finally, the best type of buyers are strategic buyers. These buyers see your business as a perfect fit into their portfolio. Perhaps they operate similar businesses in another geographic market, or maybe they operate in a complimentary service or product line in the same area. Whatever the case, they see your business as a multiplier for their business.

ADVICE FOR THE EMPLOYEE/COACH/ ADVISOR

1. Be supportive.

Selling a business is a difficult and personal decision for the business owner. Many business owners feel totally alone at this time. This is often a topic that they do not feel comfortable talking to their team about, because many of the team members may feel abandoned by their leader. They may also take it personally in that they may see their livelihood is at risk.

If they do agree to sell, then your support needs to continue with the new owners. This could be the best thing that happens for you. You do not know until it plays out.

2. Be proactive.

I had an executive coaching client who was part of an organization that was being sold. He was concerned and asked if he should leave. In this situation I knew that he was a critical member of the team. My advice to him was that he should stay. I told him that if the buyer was as sophisticated as they appeared to be, they would recognize his value and want him to stay. He heeded my advice, and not only did he stay, he was promoted multiple times over the subsequent years.

If your company does sell, do your homework. Learn about the buyer and see if they have a track record. Look for opportunities to be a key player in the organization. These are not always evident. The first thing that has to happen is a transition. Sometimes this is a very quick process, but often it takes several months and up to a year. Stepping up to help make the transition go well may open you up for new opportunities in the new organization.

I have been a part of several acquisitions and mergers. In those I have seen team members who were a critical part of the organization. In the case just mentioned, his leadership tripled the company's revenue over the next few years.

On the other hand, I have been in organizations where the team members of the acquired entity have done everything but cooperate with the new ownership. They undermined every change. They took the selling of the business personally. They sit with hands folded and are naysayers about any suggestions made. Oftentimes, these people will refer to it as a "merger" instead of an "acquisition." And, unfortunately, these situations can become a self-fulfilling prophecy. They expect to be treated unfairly, and so it happens.

CIRCLE OF (BUSINESS) LIFE

The selling and buying of businesses are a natural part of the life of any business. While it is a stressful situation for the owner, the buyer and the employees, the results can be, and often are, very positive.

Business owners should not feel that they have failed in any way when they decide to sell their business. In fact, it should be seen as a rite of passage into their next stage of life. Every business owner should have an exit strategy in mind.

I do not necessarily subscribe to the idea that you need an exit strategy when you open your business. But you should have an exit strategy while you are operating it. That strategy should include some of the basic answers. How long do I want to do this? What drivers may cause me want to sell? What do I see next for me? What do I see next for my business?

When you have an exit strategy in mind along the way, it becomes easier to put together the exit planning process when the time is right.

CTA – DO YOU HAVE AN EXIT STRATEGY?

CHAPTER 10

THERE IS NO EASY BUTTON

I started my coaching practice five years ago. Like many new business owners, my first goal was revenue. And that meant that I took any and all clients. Several of those clients were not great fits, but they gave me some experience and helped me recognize what my ideal client was.

This chapter is both a reflection on my first few years in business, as well as some examples from some of those early clients that I encountered.

When I began my business, one of the primary pieces of advice that I was given was to develop my "ideal client." This wasn't a new concept to me, as I have been exposed to sales training programs where you develop personas and humanize your target prospect.

While I agreed with the concept, I did not yet know who my ideal client would be. For example, much of my career had been in corporate IT, but I knew that they would not be a great candidate for my coaching business. (I have found most corporate IT groups to be more focused on technical skills, than soft skill development.) My more recent successes had been in smaller technology firms, but I also knew that my tenure there had been far shorter, and so I had not developed a strong reputation in that industry. I had also been working in the healthcare sector for the past several years, but I did not have any formal training there and my role had been as a vendor, not as much a healthcare professional.

I could not pinpoint a specific ideal client or industry. I decided that my practice should be founded on more of my intrinsic strengths, rather than industry-specific knowledge. So, I focused on a few ideas: entrepreneurship, business growth, and turnarounds.

I set out on this new adventure; and I landed some clients fairly quickly. Most of them came through my personal network. The first two clients I landed were friends who hired me. One was a business owner with a company that had been in business for a long time, but still hadn't been profitable. Another was the CEO of a software company who asked me to provide some sales coaching for them.

I was confident, I felt like a hero, and I was even being celebrated by my peers as someone who landed two clients quickly, right out of the gate.

But, I was not successful. In fact, I was headed down the wrong path. And while I am grateful for these initial experiences, I realize that neither of them were a great fit for what I was wanting to do.

The first was looking for a quick fix to make his company profitable. He had used some coaching in the past, but had not successfully implemented any of the concepts. We worked together for a couple of months, and I did help him in a major way. We worked on pricing strategy and developed a model that would lead to greater profitability (which it did) – but he never wanted to take on the hard tasks. He was happy that he was making a little more money, but wasn't interested in doing the things to become a world-class organization.

The second was struggling in his role and frankly was looking for answers that were fairly obvious. Their sales team was not being successful. They were leaning on marketing programs that were not delivering results. They were looking for easy ways to make the phone ring. They were throwing good money after bad, and not getting the results they wanted to see.

I'd like to say that those were the only "bad fit" clients I took on, but there have been others. One was a young entrepreneur who had purchased a company and was looking for coaching to help him grow the business. I should have caught clues during our prospecting conversations. He was asking too many questions about process and results, and talked less about where he wanted to see the business go. He signed up for bi-weekly coaching, and off we went.

I ask my clients to commit to at least three months. Coaching isn't like a vaccination, take it once and you're good for a while. Coaching is a slow progression toward a worthwhile goal, and frankly, bi-weekly coaching for three months will only get you so far. Think about it, if you have owned a business for several years, do you really think you can turn it around after only about eight hours of conversations?

Sure enough, after only four sessions — two months, this business owner broke off our engagement. He told me "things weren't happening fast enough." We had the conversation about how this takes time, but in the end, he was unwilling to commit, and I I never want to force someone to do anything.

I found out later he sold the company a few months after this. In my opinion he was more of an opportunistic business "flipper." Just like the house flipper, he bought a business that he thought he could apply some cosmetic changes to, and then sell for a tidy profit. I'm not sure that this worked out for him, and I now ask more probing questions to make sure my clients and I are a good fit.

MORE LESSONS I HAVE LEARNED

Client selection was not my only early mistake. There were many during those first two years. Another common one that I fell into was looking for marketing tools that just make the phone ring. Much like the second client mentioned earlier, who was not having success with sales.

I subscribed to several marketing services – the ones that promise that you will get hundreds or thousands of leads if you just follow their formula. Many of these use LinkedIn or other networking services. If you are on LinkedIn, I have no doubt you have been approached by some of these marketing techniques.

I realized after several months that the phone doesn't ring by itself, and that cold-calling by any other name, is still cold calling. A LinkedIn introduction with little context or an email to a stranger is as effective as knocking on doors, which means they are not very effective at all.

Another similar idea was to attend every networking event possible to build my professional network. What I found was that most events I went to were just being attended by other hungry salespeople. Most, if not all, would never purchase my services.

While my personality tendencies led me to truly enjoy my time passing out cards and getting to know other salespeople, my bank account did not see much benefit from it.

One benefit from the COVID-19 pandemic was the shut-down of many non-effective sales and marketing techniques. With no parties to attend, I found myself with more time on my hands. More importantly, it forced me to come up with more effective ways of building my business.

LOOKING FOR THE EASY WAY

So I tried several different methods. I was looking for a solution. I was looking for:

- A quick-fix to make my company profitable

- The answer to make my phone ring with prospects

- Cosmetic changes to make my company more attractive to market

- That "right" conversation at a networking event to lead to a high-dollar transaction

What did all of these approaches have in common? The answer is simple. All of these are ways of looking for what the retailer Staples called the "Easy Button." But the hard truth is this, like many of the things in life that are worthwhile, there is no such thing. Building a business is tough. It takes time, energy, money, resources, people, patience and endurance.

I was recently at a training event where the speaker kept going back to one line over and over. That after all the other planning, strategizing, visioning, and marketing, it still takes, as he would yell "MASSIVE EFFORT." He would say this with a booming voice into the microphone. Again and again reminding us that there is no "Easy Button."

A few months ago I was at a luncheon and was sitting at a table with some old friends and new acquaintances. One of them was a man that I have known for almost two decades. He has worked in several entrepreneurial businesses. Four years earlier I had met with him to discuss my idea of starting my coaching practice. At this luncheon we reflected on that conversation.

He asked, "If John of today could go back in time and join the two of us, what would he tell us?"

My answer was quick. I said "Well, I would tell him that it's going to take more time and money to get this business off the ground than you expect. And, by the way, about two years in we are going to get hit by a global pandemic that will almost ground your business to a halt for a few months."

We laughed, and then I interjected, "Nope, I take all of that back. I wouldn't want to know any of that then because I probably wouldn't have moved forward with pursuing my dream."

And that is the big lesson here for all business owners. This is hard stuff we are doing. Whether you are building a manufacturing company, bringing a new product to the market, serving in the healthcare space, selling a product or service like insurance or real estate, or simply leading a team in a large organization, the bottom line is the same. Leading is not easy. It is not for everyone. It takes MASSIVE EFFORT, and there is no Easy Button!

WHAT'S A LEADER TO DO?

If you are interested in this chapter, you are probably in a situation where the "easy" things haven't worked. You are feeling much like I was when COVID-19 started. My business was just finally starting to perform at the level I expected, and then the rug was pulled out. I realized then that I had to work smarter and harder than ever before.

Some of you just were turned off by that last statement. After all, many business owners I know originally got into business because they thought it would be easier than working for someone else. In many ways this is a valid hypothesis. The problem is that it takes time and energy to get to the point that it feels "easy." So let's explore some ideas for getting through the hard times so that we can live like there's an "easy button".

1. Develop a realistic plan.

"Expect the best, plan for the worst," the adage goes. Attributed to author and speaker Denis Waitley, he actually says, "Expect the best, plan for the worst, and expect to be surprised."".

In building a business, we must expect surprises – both positive and negative – along the way. The best way to handle them is to plan for the worst. Then, most likely, things will turn out better than you planned.

When I began my business, I sought out advice from several people. One of them was a peer of mine whom I had known for several years. He, too, was in the process of starting a new business. We shared a lot of ideas, and we still visit with each other to this day. At the time I asked him how he dealt with discouragement. You see, I had talked to several people from my corporate background who thought I was crazy to start a business. My friend shared a

> "Never ask directions from someone who hasn't been where you are going." - Unknown

piece of advice that someone else had shared with him. "Never ask directions from someone who hasn't been where you are going." I loved that! And I have stuck to that idea to this day.

After that, I turned my attention to talking to other coaches from around the world. Some of them were with FocalPoint, others were independent or with other organizations. I learned a lot from these people. One of which I heard many times, this is a tough business to get going, so plan for a long enough runway to get if off the ground.

So, that is what I did. I budgeted to take more out of savings than I originally planned. I built a growth schedule focused on an 18-to-24 month roadmap instead of six to 12 months as I had originally thought.

I read more books that year than I have ever read in my life. I watched videos and became obsessed with podcasts on topics that related to my business. If I was to become the premier business coach in my market, I had to raise my performance to an entirely new level.

I am glad that I did this, or I probably would not have made it. One of the things that FocalPoint taught me from the beginning is that every business runs into traps along the way to success. Two of the first traps we might run into are the "honeymoon trap" and the "three feet from gold" trap.

Almost every new business runs into these. Mine certainly did. Remember how I said I landed a few clients right out of the gate? The honeymoon trap is when you think those early successes are typical and easy. The reality is that they aren't, and the honeymoon will eventually be over. After landing those initial few clients, I went months before gaining any more.

The "three feet from gold" trap comes from Napoleon Hill's seminal work *Think and Grow Rich* where he talks about the prospector that gave up on his dream and sold his plot of land. The subsequent owner hit gold just three feet deeper. The message for me and other business owners is to not give up too soon. I almost did, especially when the pandemic hit.

I often now share my "pandemic story" as a message about

resilience, hope and faith. My story isn't unique, and many others have had it worse, but it was a tough road. In a matter of six weeks, four of six family members lost their jobs, my mom passed away and my business nearly collapsed. I wasn't three feet from gold. At that point I felt I was digging on the wrong plot of land! I might as well have been 300 miles from gold.

I had to fix it. And it started with fixing my mindset. I had to quit thinking like a victim and become the victor that I talked to my clients about. And one of the key parts was to establish and be loyal to my brand.

2. Build your brand.

A reality that I have learned is that everyone has a brand. If you haven't built your brand, others will build it for you. Furthermore, even when you are with a great organization like FocalPoint, your brand is *your* brand. You cannot expect to assume the brand of someone else, whether good or bad.

During the pandemic my business was almost shut down for a couple of months. It was at that time I realized that I had not really developed my brand effectively.

Up until this point I had followed several traditional methods of establishing my brand. I had profiles on all the platforms, including many you haven't heard of. I wrote blogs and produced videos on a fairly consistent basis. I had a website (a few, in fact). And I regularly shared on social media.

What I discovered is that I was not consistent in my branding choices. I shared content that sometimes was not consistent with my brand. My styles varied from being the tough, in-your-face business coach to the softer, gentler approach to helping others. My brand was inconsistent, so others made assumptions.

Some of the misperceptions were that I was primarily looking for "broken businesses." Another was that someone needed to be desperate to talk to me. It was almost like people assumed that they would come to me as a last resort to save their business.

I began rebranding myself, making sure I shared content that was more consistent. I want to make people successful, and for them to find joy in being a business owner or leader. This purpose has nothing to do with desperation or last-ditch efforts. I believe most business owners are working way too hard for much too little. So I want to help them there as well. I also want to have fun while we get there. I am not the drill sergeant business coach, hence why I am writing a book about "ugly babies." Not to be mean, but to bring a little humor to a stressful topic.

Another thing I did during the pandemic was to put on a variety of free online workshops. With almost everyone stuck in their homes, it gave me the opportunity to get in front of clients, prospects and referral partners in other ways. I focused my topics on positive topics like resilience, overcoming stress, pivoting your business and business recovery. These topics were timely, were positive, and helped build my brand as a coach who cares. People saw me living out my purpose, and not trying to be something I wasn't.

3. Leverage your network.

The final suggestion I would make is for you to work hard to leverage your existing network. I mentioned that I had spent a lot of time doing ineffective networking. I do not necessarily regret that time, because it did help me build a broader network among other professionals in my region. However, I know now that this was an ineffective way of trying to build my business.

One of my challenges was that I was somewhat stepping out from where I spent most of my career into a new arena. Many of the employees, team members, peers and clients from my past would not be the same people I called on for my new venture.

A friend and fellow FocalPoint Coach, Dan Creed, wrote a fantastic book called *Champions Don't Make Cold Calls*. Utilizing his methods, I began to focus more on my own network of champions to build my business. While I have not developed it to the level that he has, I can attest to the idea that people like to do business with people they like or admire. (Creed 2020)

So, my focus began to change. The pandemic had forced me to not rely on traditional networking "events." Many in my network even changed careers, retired or relocated during the pandemic. I communicated more with my network than I had been. I sent emails, conducted workshops and provided a lot of "free" advice.

> Knowing the right people, knowing the right people who know the people you need to know, and being known by them, can open doors that can save you years of hard work.
> **- Danny Creed, <u>Champions Never Make Cold Calls</u>**

ADVICE FOR THE EMPLOYEE/COACH/ ADVISOR

1. Keep them focused

If you are working with an entrepreneurial business owner, one of your biggest challenges is keeping them focused. We often refer to these CEOs as "chasing squirrels."

Your primary goal is to help redirect them on the most important thing. I had a client who owned a software development company that was convinced she needed a drone license. Being that she was an entrepreneur, I gave her some time to develop her idea. But when she couldn't tie it back to a reasonable idea that lined up with their strategy, we moved on to building her business in more traditional ways.

The entrepreneurial CEO needs a little rope to experiment and dream, but be prepared to reel them back when they wander too far from home.

2. Don't push for the next big thing.

I wish I had a dollar for every client who was making progress, only to then distract themselves by buying into the "next big thing." Whether this is a new marketing strategy, a new business model or a different sales tactic. Whatever it is, the next big thing is just another "thing." Some of them have merit. Some will change the world. The majority will just make you lose focus.

Some of these ideas are self-generated, like the drone example. Others are externally driven. As the advisor to your business owner, you have a chance to help filter out distractions and let the high-potential ideas through.

Before pushing a new idea to your business owner, do your research. Scrutinize it. Look at it from every perspective. Consider the tendencies of your business owner. Will they be seduced by it? Will they buy into the craze and lose traction in other areas? Be the sergeant-at-arms for your business owner's creative mind.

3. Help make the hard things easy.

Your business owner has it tough already. As has been shared in this book before, one of your greatest gifts to give is to help them be successful. Recognize the hard things they need to do. Step in and help them do these things, even when others are promoting an easier, but short-sighted, path.

When your business owner tells you something is going to be "easy", gently remind them that there is no easy button.

AND WHAT HAPPENED?

When I began to be less concerned about finding my next client, and more intent on being true to who I was, my business began to change. Referrals began coming my way. Good referrals. Referrals of people who wanted the type of help that I wanted to provide. Many companies needed to revise their strategy. Many wanted to revise their leadership styles. Others needed help with their culture.

When I look at the success I eventually had with my business, I realized that chasing the easy path was a waste of time and poor use of my energy. By addressing the three areas I shared here, I developed a profitable business that will take me through the rest of my career.

In summary, I did these not-so-simple things:

1. Expected the best, and planned for the worst
2. Developed my personal brand
3. Leveraged my network

Doing all this takes MASSIVE EFFORT. But it was worth it. And it can work for your business as well.

CTA – DO YOU HAVE AN EXIT STRATEGY?

EPILOGUE

CREATE YOUR MASTERPIECE

This past year I've had the opportunity to reflect on so many events of my career. While many of the stories I shared in this book were not necessarily the most positive memories, I cherish each one of them. They have shaped me into who I am today. By learning and growing – from mistakes and successes – I have developed a successful coaching business that allows me to help business owners and executives in avoiding some of these same mistakes.

I have learned to recognize all of these events in my life as gifts. In his book, *Positive Intelligence,* Shirzad Chamine explains that the wise perspective "accepts every outcome and circumstance as a gift and opportunity." (Chamine 2012)

There are three ways to view these experiences as gifts. They are:

> • Gifts of knowledge – We should always strive to learn from everything we do. Every experience teaches us something. Sometimes we learn what not to do. Other times we discover a better approach for the next time.

> • Gifts of strength – As the adage goes, what doesn't kill us makes us stronger. When we bounce back from adversity, we develop our mental "muscles". These muscles help us face adversity with greater courage, better attitude and genuine resilience.

- Gifts of inspiration — When adversity touches the heart, it leads us to do more. We strive to not only not repeat a mistake, but perhaps prevent it from ever happening again. Great leaders turn mistakes into inspirational actions.

More than any, the view of past adversity as a gift of inspiration has led me to developing my why. By serving these leaders, I help them *overcome their challenges and find the personal fulfilment and joy they are looking for.* Simply put, that's why I do what I do.

Like the sculptor, we take this big chunk of marble which is our life, and shave off the ugly parts and the things that don't belong. When you do that, you will find that you have created a masterpiece.

> Shave off the ugly parts and you will find yourself a masterpiece.

That's my encouragement to you today. If you find yourself at the helm of an ugly baby. Don't lose heart. Every leader has found themselves here at some point. Now is your opportunity to eliminate the ugly, and begin a new chapter. Create your masterpiece.

ACKNOWLEDGEMENTS

This book wouldn't have happened if it weren't for the encouragement of my wife of over 35 years. Debbie started saying "you should write a book," some 10-plus years ago. She has listened to my stories, given me feedback on all my writing and speaking, and encouraged me through the good times and bad. Starting my business was a dream that she was 100% apart of. I could not have done it without her. She is my rock and my encourager.

My son Joshua is as talented a writer as I know. He served as my lead editor and manuscript reviewer. He gave me feedback on much more than grammar issues (which there were plenty). His insight was profound for someone of his age. I look forward to reading his own book someday, I know it will be coming.

My daughter Katie, the quiet one of the family, reminds me all the time how important books are. She reads more than the rest of us combined. I only hope she'll pick this book up and read it to this point.

My mentor Jim Rives, who we lost just as I was beginning to work on this book. Jim always encouraged me to speak the truth to my clients, even if it was painful. If their baby was ugly, "tell them", he would say. It was the just the right thing to do.

My FocalPoint team, of which there are far too many to mention. But from Steve Thompson, Greg Pestinger and all the others who have encouraged me along the way, I truly appreciate you. I cannot imagine what it would have been like to do this journey alone.

My clients and former employers who inspired so many of the stories in this book. I appreciate every one of you. I often say the great part of coaching is that you get to experience the successes of your clients as you walk along side them. But the bad part of coaching is that you get to experience the painful lessons as you walk along side them. I am so grateful for the gift of an interesting life and to work with interesting people.

And to the Holon Publishing team. Jeremy believed in me the moment I told him the concept of this book. I appreciate your help in bringing it together. For editing, marketing, encouraging, and just being there along the way.

ABOUT THE AUTHOR

John Jennings has a passion for helping entrepreneurs, business owners and executives unlock their full potential and experience the joy and personal fulfillment of leading exceptional organizations. He has a proven track record of driving positive change in both large and small organizations. He is seen as a "turn-around guy", who credits his success to a strategic mindset and a positive attitude.

John has over two decades of IT leadership in Fortune 500 organizations such as LG&E/KU and Yum! Brands (the parent company of KFC, Taco Bell and Pizza Hut). He has also served in leadership roles for organizations of various sizes from a mid-size federal contractor to a small healthcare technology startup. Additionally, he has developed and delivered performance and leadership training in a variety of corporate and non-profit settings.

John is a certified FocalPoint Business Coach and Trainer. He chose to become a FocalPoint Business Coach because he believes strongly in their strategies, tactics and methodologies for helping people find more time, build better teams, and generate more profit.

John holds a BS degree in Computer Science from Eastern

Kentucky University and an MBA from Bellarmine University. His coaching credentials include certifications in business coaching, executive coaching, The Prioritized Leader™, Positive Intelligence™, Navigational Conversations™, and the TTI Assessments platform.

He currently serves on several non-profit boards. He is also a member of the Board of Visitors for Campbellsville University, Louisville Campus. He is active with several chamber groups, including Greater Louisville, Inc.'s Health Enterprises Network and is the leadership development partner for the Jeffersontown (Ky) Chamber of Commerce. He has been an active leader in the Boy Scouts, serving in local, district and council-level leadership roles.

If you would like to speak to John, find him at
www.johnkjennings.com
or connect with him on LinkedIn at
https://linkedin.com/in/johnkjennings.

REFERENCES

Chamine, Shirzad. 2012. Positive Intelligence: *Why only 20% of Teams and Individuals Achieve Their True Potential AND HOW YOU CAN ACHIEVE YOURS.* Greenleaf Book Group Press.

Creed, Danny. 2020. *Champions Never Make Cold Calls*. Camas, WA: The Publishing Circle.

Dannemiller, K. D., & Jacobs, R. W. 1992. "Changing the way organizations change: A revolution of common sense." T*he Journal of Applied Behavioral Science* 480–498.

Eduard Spranger, Ronald Bonnstetter, Bill J. Bonnstetter. 2013 (original 1928). *Types of Men.* Target Training International, Ltd.

Kruger, Justin, and David Dunning. 1999. "Unskilled and Unaware of It: How Difficulties in Recognizing One's Own Incompetence Lead to Inflated Self-Assessments." *Journal of Personality and Social Psychology.*

McHugh, Adam. 2015. "The Listening Life." In The Listening Life, by Adam McHugh. IVP Books.

Sinek, Simon. 2019. "The Infinite Game." *In The Infinite Game*, by Simon Sinek. Penguin Random House, LLC.

Spears, L.C. (Ed.). 1998. Insights on leadership: Service, stewardship, spirit and servant-leadership. New York, NY: John Wiley & Sons.

Tracy, Brian. n.d. *Power of Personal Achievement*. Brian Tracy International.

TTI. 2018. "10 Ways to Increase Your Emotional Intelligence."

TTI Success Insights. n.d. *TTI Success Insights.* Accessed June 1, 2018. https://www.ttisi.com/.

Wason, Peter. 1972. *"Psychology of Reasoning: Structure and Content."* In *Psychology of Reasoning: Structure and Content,* by Wason with P N Johnson-Laird. Accessed June 1, 2021.

https://www.life.church/leadershippodcast/winning-the-war-in-your-mind-cognitive-biases/.